Joshua Girling Fitch

Notes on American Schools And Training Colleges

Joshua Girling Fitch

Notes on American Schools And Training Colleges

ISBN/EAN: 9783744723916

Printed in Europe, USA, Canada, Australia, Japan

Cover: Foto ©Thomas Meinert / pixelio.de

More available books at **www.hansebooks.com**

NOTES ON AMERICAN SCHOOLS AND TRAINING COLLEGES

REPRINTED FROM THE REPORT OF THE ENGLISH EDUCATION DEPARTMENT FOR 1888-89 WITH THE PERMISSION OF THE CONTROLLER OF H. M. STATIONERY OFFICE

BY

J. G. FITCH, M.A., LL.D.

ONE OF HER MAJESTY'S CHIEF INSPECTORS OF TRAINING COLLEGES

London

MACMILLAN AND CO.

AND NEW YORK

1890

INTRODUCTION.

THE occasion of the appearance of these " Notes " will be best explained by quoting the following extract from my annual official report on English Training Colleges, presented to Parliament in 1889:

"Through the favor of your Lordships, I was permitted last year to extend the usual official holiday, and so to gratify a wish which I had long entertained, to visit some of the leading schools and colleges in America. I have appended to this report, in the form of some notes, such of the chief facts and considerations brought under my notice in the course of this journey as I thought most likely to prove interesting and suggestive to school managers, masters, and mistresses at home, especially to those who are concerned in the training of elementary teachers."

This sentence indicates, I hope, with sufficient clearness, the very limited scope and pretensions of the notes which are here reprinted. A full and exhaustive account of so complex a subject as American Education would have been impossible in the very brief time at my disposal. And it was mainly to furnish hints and information to my own countrymen, and not with a view to tell the American public anything which they did not know before, that these notes were written. Nevertheless, since a wish has been expressed by some of my many Transatlantic friends that what I have here said should be reprinted in the "States," my consent to that course has been willingly given; and the more willingly because to the real sympathy and admiration with which I witnessed some of the chief educational phenomena in America, there is added in this instance a very deep sense of the generous and thoughtful attention which I everywhere received from those whose institutions I visited or whose help I sought.

To institute comparisons of the methods, the extent, or the results of educational work in Europe and in America would be presumptuous without a much fuller acquaintance with the interior life of schools and colleges than it would be possible for a visitor to obtain. And as to mere figures, statistics, and printed reports, they may prove seriously misleading, unless the special conditions which give their true significance to those details are thoroughly understood. If I needed a warning against indulging in hasty generalizations from *data* imperfectly understood, I should find it in a recent article, otherwise very weighty and suggestive, which appeared under the honored name of Dr. Edward

Everett Hale in the *Forum* of July last. In it the writer says :

"We spend more on public education in America than has been spent upon it in Great Britain in twenty years. In the year 1886, which I select for comparison because it is the latest in ' Whitaker's Almanack,' the State of Massachusetts alone, with a population of less than 2,000,000 people, expended about $6,000,000 for the public education of its children, while the kingdom of Great Britain, with a population of 35,000,000, expended only $17,000,-000 in the same time. *What follows, of course, is that there are twenty times as many readers in America in the same population as there are in England.*"

The misleading character of the statement here, and the fallacy of the remarkable inference which is deduced from it, and which I have printed in italic, will be evident on considering two things :

(1) The figures quoted by Dr. Hale represent the parliamentary grant for elementary education only; that is to say, for children presumably of the laboring class, whose education is not prolonged beyond the fourteenth year, and who are supposed to need the assistance of a public fund in order to procure the means of education. No grant is made by Parliament for the instruction of children of the middle and upper classes who do not use the public elementary schools, nor for advanced or high-school instruction for pupils of any class;

whereas the Massachusetts fund provides for higher and intermediate, as well as for purely elementary education, and the public schools are attended by the children of all classes of the community.

(2) The statistics presented in Dr. Hale's article are from the official returns of the Education Department. But that Department simply administers a "grant in aid" of local effort. The sum annually voted by Parliament for elementary education is only a part, and not the largest part, of the fund available even for that limited purpose. During the year referred to, in which $17,000,000 in the form of grants from the Imperial Exchequer were appropriated to elementary schools, the contributions of parents in the shape of fees to the same schools amounted to $8,500,000, the voluntary subscriptions to $3,500,000, the local rates to $5,500,000, and other resources to $500,000, thus making a total revenue of $35,000,000 for the elementary schools alone; whereas the figures quoted for Massachusetts represent the entire school fund, which is not, so far as I can ascertain, supplemented by contributions either from parents or from other sources.

Indeed, there is little or no analogy between the educational systems in a young community which has found itself unhampered by traditions, and free to fashion new institutions; and those of a country like England, in which educational systems

INTRODUCTION.

—if so they may be called—are unsymmetrical, and are the outcome of compromise and of historical development. As I have in another place* had occasion to say, "It is very characteristic of this country, of its genius, its traditions, its history, and the idiosyncrasies of its people, that many of its most cherished institutions are the result of growth rather than of manufacture ; have not been consciously predetermined by legislators or by theorists, but have shaped themselves by a process of slow evolution to suit the changed circumstances and needs of successive generations." This general statement is strikingly verified in the history of education in England, and in the character of the provision now made for sustaining it.

For example : secondary and intermediate education is in England provided wholly by voluntary, local, or private effort, and has never yet been directed or subsidized by the central government. There is, therefore, no organized system of public instruction extending beyond the requirements of children who leave school for work in their thirteenth or fourteenth year. An increasing number of the secondary schools of England are established at the instance of local committees or of public bodies, such as the Girls' Public Day School Company, or are the result of the combined efforts of the parents. Such schools, when established, are generally placed under

---

* In the article " Education," in *Chambers's Cyclopædia*.

INTRODUCTION.

the supervision of responsible governing bodies, and are annually subjected to examination by the Universities or other public authority. But the most important part of the provision for secondary education is supplied by Endowed schools, to which in England the name "grammar school" is generally given. Many of these foundations date back to the time of the Reformation, some of them still inherit revenues originally transferred from the monastic institutions which were dissolved early in the sixteenth century; and many others owe their origin to the testaments and deeds of gift of munificent founders. These foundation schools were chiefly designed for instruction in Latin and Greek. They are scattered throughout the whole country, and over all of them the State, as the supreme trustee of all endowments for public purposes, has from time to time exercised, though to a very limited extent, its right of supervision. But they have not been coördinated or subjected to any general scheme of public instruction. The legislation of 1869 has empowered a Commission to frame schemes for the reconstitution of the governing bodies, for releasing those bodies from the obligation to obey antiquated and unworkable regulations, and for modernizing and improving the courses of study. It is a conspicuous feature of all these schemes that by them a substantial part of the endowment is reserved for the purpose of helping meritorious scholars to obtain gratuitous educa-

INTRODUCTION.

tion, either by securing for them free places on the foundation, or by means of scholarships and exhibitions enabling the holders to proceed to the Universities or other places of higher education. But with these exceptions, no public fund in England is available for instruction in secondary and higher schools ; and the parents of children in such schools are always required to pay the full cost of the education they obtain.

And the relation of the central government in England to the primary instruction of the laboring classes differs essentially from that which exists either in the States of the American Union or in any country in Europe. Till near the middle of this century the only means available for such instruction were provided by educational societies, by the churches, or by private philanthropy. It was in 1832 that Parliament voted, by way of experiment, a small annual sum of £20,000 for the building of schools, and intrusted the distribution of the fund to the two educational societies which had been founded by the supporters of Dr. Bell and Joseph Lancaster. In 1839 a Committee of Council was formed for the administration of a rather larger sum for the maintenance of schools, and in 1846 a more elaborate scheme of grants in aid of voluntary schools was organized. But until the Act of 1870 no other primary schools existed in England except those established at the instance and on the responsibility of voluntary bodies. In that year

Parliament for the first time accepted, as a national obligation, the duty of providing schools, and enacted that wherever the existing provision of efficient voluntary schools was inadequate, it should be incumbent on the district to establish a School Board and to supply the deficiency by means of a local rate. But from the first the principle adopted by the legislature has been that the State should begin by recognizing the agency of all efficient voluntary and religious bodies, and should seek their coöperation. The Department of the State intrusted with the duty of administering the parliamentary grant was not called into existence for the purpose of imposing on the nation its own educational theories, or of prescribing in all cases what should be learned or how it should be taught. It was charged with the distribution of a sum of public money in aid of local effort, leaving to school managers, whether elected Boards or voluntary Committees, the fullest freedom of administration and initiative in regard to the choice of teachers and the processes of instruction. At the same time it necessarily reserved to itself the power to lay down the conditions under which the grant shall be obtained, and to proportion the amount of that grant to the number of the scholars and to the efficiency of the schools. Accordingly, regulations are laid down describing the minimum of school accommodation and equipment, and of the staff of qualified teachers which will entitle a school

INTRODUCTION. 11

to recognition; and a programme, both of obligatory and of optional subjects, is issued to indicate the character of the educational results, which will be taken into account in computing the grant. To this extent, and to this extent only, can the Government of Great Britain be said to control public instruction, or to have an educational system at all.

These facts, so familiar to my own countrymen, are here recounted, partly with a view to show to American readers the very exceptional conditions which dominate the organization of English education, and mainly in order to explain the point of view from which an English official is likely to look at the whole problem, and to observe the spirited and well-devised measures by which America is seeking to solve it.

December, 1889.

NOTES ON AMERICAN SCHOOLS
AND TRAINING COLLEGES.

THOSE who would understand the educational institutions of America must first give heed to the exceptional conditions under which these institutions originated and still continue to work. The American Republic is a unique organization. It differs essentially from France, in which the several departments are mere local administrative areas, with little or no political autonomy, and form together a nation, "one and indivisible," controlled and regulated at Paris as the capital and centre of the national life. It is somewhat less unlike the Swiss Federation. The acts of the several cantons of Switzerland derive all their validity from the Federal Government at Berne. The "Pact" of 1803 defines the several powers of the League and of the cantonal governments, and gives much larger powers to the former than belong to the Federal Government at Washington. America is, as Mr. Bryce has well de-

Special conditions existing in the American Union.

scribed it, "a commonwealth of commonwealths, a republic of republics, a State which, while one, is nevertheless composed of other States even more essential to its existence than it is to theirs." The States are older than the Union. "The Constitution of 1789 turned a league of States into a Federal State by giving it a national Government with a direct authority over all the citizens." But the nature of this authority was strictly defined and limited, and did not supersede the governments of the several States. Each community retained many of the attributes of a sovereign State, and while parting with such rights as those of coining money, maintaining an army, making treaties and the like—rights which belong to the nation in its corporate capacity, secured for herself by Article 1 of the Constitution complete independence in regard to all matters of internal administration. "The powers vested in each State are all of them original and inherent powers which belonged to the State before it entered the Union. Hence they are *primâ facie* unlimited, and, if a question arises as to any particular power, it is presumed to be enjoyed by the State unless it can be shown to have been taken away by the Federal Constitution, or, in other words, a State is not deemed to be subject to any restriction which the Constitution has not distinctly imposed." (Bryce's *American Commonwealth*, I. 424.)

Among the prerogatives of an independent and

AND TRAINING COLLEGES. 15

autonomous Government, with which the States have not parted, and are not likely to part, is the absolute control of public education. There is, therefore, no national or American system, but a number of separate systems. Each State has its own educational laws, and raises, appropriates, and distributes school funds in its own way.

Education essentially a matter for the States, not for the Union.

There is, it is true, at Washington, a central Bureau of Education, which was founded in 1867, and which is maintained by Congress at an annual charge of about $50,000. It is intrusted with the duty of collecting statistics and publishing and circulating information; but it has no authority. It cannot even enforce the production of figures or information, or impose any regulation or principle of action on the legislature of any State. The commissionership has during twenty years been held by three distinguished men, Henry Barnard, General Eaton, and N. H. Dawson, and an energetic commissioner may secure for his office a good deal of indirect influence by the publication of reports and of useful monographs, the work of skilled writers in special departments of educational work. The Bureau also gathers together, chiefly for the information of members of Congress, numerous memoirs and reports respecting the educational systems in foreign countries, and is forming by degrees a valuable educational library. But it is in no sense a controlling or even an advising body,

The Washington Bureau.

NOTES ON AMERICAN SCHOOLS

and its existence is hardly recognized by the local educational authorities in the several States.

In one respect only has the central Government concerned itself with education. In 1785 it was ordained that in all new States hereafter to be added to the 17 then existing, a special appropriation of one-sixteenth of the public land should be reserved for the purpose of supplying a school fund. There are now 42 States in the American Union, but many of them sold the lands in order to defray the initial charge of erecting schools, and comparatively few now enjoy the rent or use it as a permanent revenue for maintenance of the schools. They all require further aid from State or local taxation. The State of Indiana has the distinction of having husbanded its resources with exceptional discretion and ability, and its last report shows that out of a total school revenue of $1,657,703 about $1,000,000 were derived from property, $449,979 from local taxation, and $204,985 from liquor licenses, and other minor sources. As a rule, however, the annual charge to be met by local assessment is much higher than in this case.

Provision of public lands for education.

The relations of the several provinces in Canada to the Dominion Government are closely analogous to those of the States of the American Union to the Federal Government. Neither in the States nor in the Dominion is there any centralized system.

Resemblance between the States of the Union and the provinces of the Canadian Dominion.

AND TRAINING COLLEGES.

Hence there are considerable diversities in the character of the educational arrangements in different parts of the North American continent. An enterprising and liberal community may make, and often does make, ample provision for sumptuous school buildings and an ambitious course of instruction. But if a local educational authority chooses to accept a narrow and poor ideal of education, or to make grudging and insufficient appropriation of public money for its support; if, for example, its law is satisfied with country schools which are open only six or even four months in the year or contains no provision for enforcing attendance, there is no central authority which can exercise any influence upon it, or which is entitled to declare that the educational provision is insufficient.

Here, for example, is a very significant extract from the last official report from the State of Alabama :

"In point of material resources and natural advantages Alabama is surpassed by no State in the Union. . . If in our haste to grow rich we neglect our public school system and the moral training of our youth, these natural advantages and boundless resources may become a snare to us. . . But if we foster our public school system, as many of our sister States have done, we shall be blessed with a thrifty, enterprising class of immigrants, who will appreciate free public schools, and who will invest their money among us and heartily co-operate with us in developing our State and in perpetuating our free institutions. To such a class of immigrants a public school system that pays no more than $1 per child, including poll-tax ; that pays teachers on an average only $21.87 per month ; that runs its free public schools only 70½ days in the year, and that does not pretend to provide any school buildings, is not very inviting."

In one respect, at least, the public school system throughout the Union is uniform. It is entirely secular, and no church or religious body as such has even an indirect control over the external or internal management of the common school. It is not unusual for the school-work to begin with a short religious exercise—a hymn, the Lord's Prayer, and a reading from the Scriptures "without written note or oral comment," and the public law of Massachusetts prescribes that :

The common schools in the States always secular.

" It shall be the duty of all preceptors and teachers of academies, and of all other instructors of youth, to exert their best endeavors to impress on the minds of children and youth committed to their care and instruction, the principles of piety and justice and a sacred regard to truth, love of their country, humanity and universal benevolence ; sobriety, industry and frugality ; chastity, moderation and temperance ; and those other virtues which are the ornament of human society, and the basis

AND TRAINING COLLEGES.

on which a republican constitution is founded: and it shall be the duty of such instructors to endeavor to lead their pupils, as their ages and capacities will admit, into a clear understanding of the tendency of the above-named virtues to preserve and perfect a republican constitution and secure the blessings of liberty as well as to promote their future happiness, and also to point out to them the evil tendency of the opposite vices."

These injunctions, however, are merely general. Neither in the time tables and schemes of instruction for Boston, nor in those of any State or city, have I found provision for Bible reading by the scholars, or for religious teaching in any form.

For this and for other reasons the public school system, though theoretically comprehensive, does not extend to all the children of school age. On the one hand, the Roman Catholic Church and some members of the Episcopal and other churches desire for their children definite religious instruction, and make considerable sacrifices in order to maintain denominational schools in efficiency. On the other hand, many of the richer people dislike the publicity and the associations of the common schools, and prefer to educate their children at their own cost in private establishments. In the city of Philadelphia 110,000 scholars are to be found in the public schools, and 30,000 are taught in the schools of religious bodies or of private teachers. In Boston it is computed that five-sixths of all the scholars under instruction are in public and one-sixth in private establishments. In the city of New York the proportion of scholars withdrawn either on religious or on social grounds from the public schools is said to be increasing. No supervision of any kind is exercised by the local governments over the private and denominational schools. They are not inspected, except for sanitary purposes; their teachers are not required to hold any certificate of qualification, and they receive no aid whatever from public funds. In districts in which the Catholic influence has become powerful a desire is often strongly expressed to adopt so much of the English system as will allow the religious schools to receive pecuniary help, and to be recognized as part of the provision for public instruction on giving due evidence of efficiency in regard to secular teaching. But at present no State or city has yielded to this demand. Indeed, the question is often discussed whether, having regard to the terms and to the spirit of the Federal Constitution, and to the absolute religious equality which that instrument secures to the community, it is within the power of any single State to make grants of public money to schools under the management of clerical bodies. The question has not been authoritatively settled ; and whenever it takes a practical shape, and any State or city seriously proposes to accept the co-operation of the churches and to subsidize denominational schools, a very

AND TRAINING COLLEGES.

grave and acrimonious controversy may be expected
to arise and to excite interest throughout all the
States of the Union.

No such difficulty about the recognition of denominational schools exists in Canada. But not in
Under the British North America Act Canada.
of 1867 the supporters of separate schools were
guaranteed certain privileges which the local legislature may extend but may not abridge. Thus, in
Ontario or Upper Canada, though the public school
system is undenominational, the Protestant separate
and the Roman Catholic separate schools are recognized as adjuncts to it, and receive grants and regular
inspection under the Minister of Public Instruction.
In the province of Quebec or Lower Canada the
Council of Public Instruction is composed of Roman Catholic ecclesiastics and laymen and of Protestant members. These are divided into two committees, Protestant and Catholic, and the school
funds raised by taxation are divided between the
two bodies and between the schools of the two
classes in proportion to the population. There are
Protestant Inspectors and Catholic Inspectors, and
the two committees regulate the choice of books
and the system of instruction for their respective
schools. There is, therefore, in this province, and
especially in the city of Quebec, in which the proportion of French Catholics is large and increasing,
an essentially denominational system ; and Catholic
schools and teachers enjoy a larger share of public

recognition and of material help from public funds than in any Catholic country in Europe.

Throughout the American Union, although each State has its own educational authority, the practical working of the school system is left to the *Local administrative bodies.* school boards or to the committees of smaller administrative areas, such as the county or the township. Every large city, also, has its own school committee, makes from the local taxation its own appropriation of money, appoints its own officials, issues its own licenses to practise, and its own regulations and schemes of instruction. For all practical purposes the organization of public instruction in Boston or Chicago is as independent of the State authority of Massachusetts or Illinois as if the city happened to be situated in another State.

The local authorities or school boards are very differently constituted. In some cases they are nominated by the governor of the State, in others by the mayor of the city, or by the judges. In one town the body of aldermen constitutes the school committee. In other cases there is direct popular election *ad hoc*. But all the local committees, however constituted, are more or less the product of political influences, and are subject to frequent changes. One hears frequent lamentations over the personal incompetence of many of the members of such committees to serve as efficient directors of education; and over the manner in which

AND TRAINING COLLEGES. 23

patronage is abused and appointments of teachers are made through personal interest and favor. Especially it is urged, with some truth, that the constant changes in the composition of the boards render it difficult to pursue a continuous policy or to develop the school system on a fixed plan. There is little or no comity among the several educational authorities, scarcely any interchange of teachers, and little opportunity for comparison of experience, except by purely voluntary associations.

Notwithstanding this diversity of organization, there are certain general resemblances in the plans of instruction throughout the States. The chief features which they possess in common are the following :

General features of the school systems.

The period of elementary education is from 6 to 14. The schools are divided into *primary* departments, which receive children from 6 to 10 ; and *grammar* departments, in which the scholars range from 10 to 14. Each division is subdivided into classes or *grades*. In schools in the great cities there are often 12 or 14 grades, some of which represent half-yearly courses of instruction ; in most of the schools there are, between the ages of 6 and 14, eight yearly courses or grades ; while in small ungraded schools in the country, although the scholars of advanced age are expected to show greater proficiency, a classification into two or three groups for purposes of collective instruction is recognized.

Classification by age, though not rigidly insisted on,* is more common than in our schools. At the end of each period the .scholars are examined for promotion, sometimes by their own teachers, more often by the school superintendent and his Inspectors, and the scholar who is not successful remains in the lower class, otherwise he is expected to be found in the class appropriate to his age. The liberty of classification enjoyed by English teachers, which enables them so often to place in the First Standard, appropriate to the eighth year, new scholars of 10 or even 11 years of age, could not, as a rule, be exercised in America, except at the risk of censure.

In the pages appended to these notes I have summarized the official requirements for the grades

---

* This sentence has been much criticised, though not refuted, by some of our teachers at home. It simply records the undoubted fact that, so far as my observation extended, the ages of American scholars corresponded more nearly to the "grade" or class in which they were placed, than the ages of children to the appropriate "standards" in English elementary schools. On the question of the right basis of classification I have here expressed no opinion. But I have no doubt that while it would be absurd and pedantic to place children in classes solely on the ground of the differences in their age, there is no good school of any rank, from Eton down to the humblest pauper school, in which teachers do not take into account the age of the pupil as one important factor in determining the class in which he is to be placed, besides their estimate of his ability and attainments.

AND TRAINING COLLEGES. 25

corresponding to the English standards, taken from several local regulations. They may be regarded as fairly typical. An English boy who goes through the course with credit up to 14 is said to have passed the Seventh Standard. An American boy who reached the same point would be said to have "graduated" in the grammar school.

Above the grammar school many States and cities provide high schools. These furnish an education adapted to scholars from 14 or 15 to 18. The admirable high schools at Boston, the English and the Latin, described with such strong appreciation in the report of the late Bishop (then Mr.) Fraser in 1866, continue to flourish and to offer a generous and stimulating course of instruction in language and history, science and mathematics. The "elective" system under which the parents are at liberty to take so much of the programme as may suit the special aptitudes and destination of their children prevails largely in the high schools as in the universities of America. The following programme of the Washington High School will serve as a characteristic illustration of the aims and plans of some of the best schools of that class :

NOTES ON AMERICAN SCHOOLS

WASHINGTON HIGH SCHOOL.

Three Courses of Study outlined.

YEAR.	ACADEMIC.	SCIENTIFIC.	BUSINESS.
First.	English. History. Algebra. Latin. Physiology. Physical Geography. } Lectures.	English. History. Algebra. German. Physiology. Physical Geography. } Lectures.	English. History. Algebra. Book-keeping and Business Arithmetic. Physiology. Physical Geography. } Lectures.
Second.	*English* (1st half year), *History* and *Political Economy* (2d half year). Geometry. Latin. Physics or Greek.	English (1st half year), History and Political Econ'my (2d half year), or Chemistry (whole year). Geometry. German. Physics.	English (1st half year), History and Political Econ'my (2d half year), or Chemistry (whole year). Book-keeping and Business Arithmetic. Commercial Law and Commercial Geography. Physics.
Third.	Trigonometry and Surveying or English. Latin. *French* or *Greek.* *Botany.* *Chemistry* and *Mineralogy.* *History* and *Political Economy.* *Advanced Physics.*	Trigonometry and Surveying or English. German. *French.* *Botany.* *Chemistry* and *Mineralogy.* *History* and *Political Economy.* *Advanced Physics.*	Diplomas given at the end of two years, but graduates desiring to continue in school may take suitable studies of third year in other courses.

AND TRAINING COLLEGES. 27

(*a*) Elective studies are printed in *italics ;* all others are prescribed.

(*b*) General exercises in composition, declamation or reading, and drawing are required in all the courses ; a general exercise in music is optional.

(*c*) Instruction in a mechanical workshop is provided for selected students from each of the boys' classes.

(*d*) Not more than four studies may be pursued at one time.

(*e*) Candidates for diplomas must pursue all the prescribed studies of the first and second years, and at least three studies in the third year ; students who from any cause fail to meet this requirement are enrolled as "unclassified."

It should be observed that the American high school is unlike any institution in England. It is essentially a continuation school, and is in close organic connection with the primary or grammar schools. It does not receive pupils till the age of 14, and all its arrangements pre-suppose that, before entering it, the pupil has gone successfully through the "grammar" grades. An English "grammar school" or middle school exists side by side with a public elementary school, but has no relation to it. The latter takes scholars from 6 or 7 to 14, and the former from 7 or 8 to 17 or 18. The two are attended by scholars of very different social ranks, and each has its own course of instruction fashioned from the first on the theory that the course will extend to a certain age, and that this course must, in view of that fact, have a completeness of its own. The broader and more liberal aims of the English grammar school affect the character of the daily lessons from the first. Subjects are begun in it by the age of 10 or

Difference between an American high school and an English grammar or intermediate school.

11 which do not come into the curriculum of the elementary school at all. Hence if by means of scholarships or otherwise a boy of promise is to be taken from the lower school to the higher, it is necessary to choose him early, say at 11 or 12, and to transfer him to the one from the other at once. He would not derive the full advantage of the higher school course if he stayed to complete the seven standards of the elementary school. But in America the "ladder" is differently constructed. The end of the grammar school curriculum coincides with the beginning of that of the high school. Both schools are generally under the same management. And, except for the fact that it is the poorer parent who is compelled to withdraw his child earliest for labor, both are attended by the same class of pupils. Hence a good deal of the waste of power in England, owing to the separation of children of different social ranks into distinct schools during the period of purely elementary education is avoided. Our "higher" schools are higher, not because they are occupied in doing advanced work, nor because relatively to the needs of a scholar in the early stage of his education they are giving better elementary instruction, but partly because they contemplate the extension of the studies to a later age, and mainly because they are attended by pupils whose parents are rich enough to pay for their education, and therefore do not need the help of a Government grant.

AND TRAINING COLLEGES.

The supply of high schools is not uniform throughout the country. They are to be found in most though not all of the great cities. The public school law of Massachusetts requires a high school whenever the place contains 500 children of school age ; and that State contains no less than 229 high schools. The public school system of the city of New York includes no high school. The place of such an institution is partly supplied by the College of the City of New York, which gives a scientific and literary training to young men, and partly by the Normal school for young women—which is not, as its name seems to imply, an institution wholly for the training of teachers, since its lower classes give a good general education, and since many scholars enter it without any intention of proceeding to the higher departments in which special professional training is given to future schoolmistresses. When it is considered that instruction in all the schools which are once incorporated into the public school system is gratuitous, it is not a little remarkable that the proportion of scholars availing themselves of this provision is so small. In Chicago, for example, a prosperous city of 875,000 inhabitants, amply supplied with excellent schools, there are only 2,000 scholars in the high schools, of whom less than 500 are boys ; and of these it is computed that less than half remain long enough to complete the course. In Boston, a city in which the appreciation of knowledge and culture has long been exceptionally high, the elementary schools are attended in all by 55,451 scholars, of whom 2,211 are in the highest class and 3,429 are in the second class, corresponding to our 7th and 6th Standards respectively. The grammar school diploma was in 1887 awarded to 1,992 "graduates." This gives a proportion of scholars successfully completing the elementary school course in a given year of about one twenty-eighth of the whole number of pupils, and, assuming an average stay in the schools of seven years, this points roughly to the conclusion that one-fourth of the scholars will probably proceed to the end of the course. In the same year the schools of the London School Board are reported to have presented 264,791 scholars for examination in standards, of whom 6,379 were in and above the 7th Standard, a number not amounting to one-fortieth of the whole, and suggesting that if seven years be the ordinary length of the school life, not many more than one-sixth of the scholars now in board schools will remain long enough to complete their course by passing in Standard VII. Considering, however, that the scholars in the London board schools belong almost all to the wage-earning class, and that those of the Boston public schools include the children of persons of all social grades, the comparison is nowise unfavorable. If we had, as in Boston, statistics showing the total number of scholars of all ranks who remained under instruc-

AND TRAINING COLLEGES.

tion till 13, 14, and 15 respectively, it may be doubted whether London would appear at any disadvantage. Yet the statistics of Boston give a higher average of scholars in advanced schools and classes than those of any other city in the States, whose figures I have had an opportunity of examining. Of the 1,992 who "graduated" in the Boston grammar schools, 1,081, or 54 per cent., subsequently entered either the English or the Latin high schools. This fact represents a very satisfactory proportion. But applying the same test, and by taking into account the numbers who reach the advanced class in the high schools, it appears that little more than one-fifth complete the four years' course and become "graduates" of the high school.

Indeed, a comparison of the general statistics of school attendance in America with those of our own country cannot fairly be made without keeping in view the fact that here the public elementary schools are designed for the children of the laboring class, and are not used except to a very small extent by parents above that class. But the educational returns of America extend to the children of all the classes who attend public schools at all. It should also be borne in mind that according to the latest returns the population of the United States (57,929,609) is, roughly speaking, about double that of England and Wales. In the light of these facts the following figures are significant : The report of 1887 of

Comparison of English and American school attendance.

the Commissioner of Education shows the number of scholars on the rolls in all the public schools to be 11,805,660, and the average number in daily attendance to be 7,571,416, or 64 per cent. In the report of the English Education Department for last year 4,635,184 were enrolled on the registers of the elementary schools of England and Wales; of whom 3,527,381, or 76 per cent., were in average daily attendance. This average, it must be observed, is computed in England on a minimum of 400 school attendances, or 200 days, in the ·year. But in many parts of America the schools are open less than half this number of times. For example: In the State of Connecticut, which is said to take the lead in regard to the enforcement of attendance, the law is satisfied with 120 days' attendance in the year; and in many districts of that State schools are open only for six months in the year. The average term of the school in the State of Mississippi was 84 days in the year 1887. In the State of New York the Act requires 14 weeks of school attendance in the year. The new compulsory law of 1887 for the State of Maine, which is designed to supersede the less stringent regulations hitherto in force, requires attendance for 16 weeks in the year.

One obvious conclusion from these returns is that the system of free schools does not necessarily · secure a high average of regularity in attendance. There are compulsory laws in several of the great

AND TRAINING COLLEGES.

cities, and truant officers whose business it is to enforce them ; but they are in most cases very leniently administered, and in many towns, and over large tracts of country, they do not exist at all. It is the experience of all school authorities that wherever wages are high, and there are many openings for juvenile labor, the children drop off in great numbers at 11 and 12 years of age ; and that there are no public measures which are effective enough to prevent it. The rule which so often prevails in the states of Germany, requiring attendance at a continuation school or *Fortbildungs Schule* in the case of all scholars who fail to reach a certain standard in the ordinary day schools at 13 or 14, has no force in the American States. Statistics of actual illiteracy have not been compiled in such a way as to furnish data for any comprehensive induction ; but those of several States may be usefully compared. In the State of Massachusetts the last report computed that there were, in 1885, 122,263 "illiterates," forming 7.73 per cent. of the population. Of these, 6.79 per cent. were born in Massachusetts, 4.58 in other States, and 88.63 per cent. were foreign born. These figures include illiterates of all ages, many of whom have come into the State after reaching maturity. If only the minors from 10 to 20 are considered, they will be found to be only 9.92 of the total number as against 11.99 in 1875. This is one of the most favorable statements, and shows how very large a part of the ignorance

3

34　NOTES ON AMERICAN SCHOOLS

and poverty of the New England States is imported. But other figures offer a striking contrast. In Alabama, out of a population of 1,262,505, no less than 433,447 over the age of 10 were unable to write. Michigan, with a much more generous school system, had, out of a population of 1,648,690, only 63,672 illiterates; and Arkansas, out of a population of 1,542,359, had 410,722.

In regard to the material fabric of the schools generally, only two or three facts need to be mentioned. The teaching is conducted in separate class-rooms, but provision is nearly always made for one hall large enough to contain the whole of the pupils, and available for collective exercises, and for the annual prize giving and other ceremonials. In some instances both of these objects are fulfilled in the same apartment. At a large school in New York I saw several hundred scholars assembled for the opening exercise and singing, and immediately afterwards a number of partitions, which had been ingeniously attached to the roof, descended at a signal, and the whole of the large hall was at once transformed into a number of separate class-rooms. The schools generally are less amply furnished with playgrounds than schools of corresponding grades in England; and it seemed to me that much less use was made of them during the mid-day recess. Some of the elementary schools, especially in New York, were too crowded for health or comfort. The offi-

The school buildings and furniture.

AND TRAINING COLLEGES.

cial regulations issued by the City Superintendent prescribe the following as the minimum of floor-space and air-space per pupil : "In the three lower classes of the primary schools, five square feet and seventy cubic feet ; in the three higher grades, six square and eighty cubic feet; in the four lower grades of grammar schools, seven square feet and ninety cubic feet, and in the four higher grades, nine square feet and one hundred cubic feet per scholar." Space, however, is exceptionally valuable in the city of New York, and these *minima* are generally exceeded in other places. The plan of seating pupils at single separate desks is common and has many advantages; but it does not economize space well. It fills a room with desks, so that there is no space for collective movement or for causing the class to vary its position by occasional standing ; and if the numbers are large the scholars are spread over so wide an area that the teacher's voice is needlessly tried.

One very useful mechanical device, which is not without an important incidental effect on the whole character of the teach-ing, is to be found in nearly all the best American schools. It is the continuous blackboard, or black-ened surface extending all round the room, after the fashion of what house painters here call a "dado." I am frequently struck in England with the waste of power caused by the smallness of the blackboard surface accessible to the teacher. More

than half of what is written or drawn in illustration
of the lessons I hear at home is rubbed out directly,
and before it has served its purpose, simply because
room is wanted to write or draw something else.
English teachers have yet to learn the proper use of
a blackboard. There is much waste of time whenever anything is sketched or written upon it, and
not afterwards read or referred to, and made an
effective instrument of recapitulation. Unless the
questions, " What have I written here ? " " Why
did I write it ? " " What is the meaning of this
diagram ? " " Can you explain it to the class ? "
occur later in the lesson, the board should not be
used at all. Nor unless the series of demonstra-
tions, examples, or pictures remain within sight of
the learner during the whole of the lesson, and for
a time afterwards, is it possible for him to go back
and get a clear notion of the right order of its development, or to see any continuity or wholeness in
it. An American teacher generally understands
this. He begins at one end of the wall behind his
estrade and goes on to the other end ; erasing nothing, but letting all the parts of his subject be illustrated in order, and referring back to them from
time to time. And at the end of his lesson he sends
some of the scholars to the side walls to work out
in the presence of the class other problems, to reproduce a diagram, or to write an illustrative sentence. There is plenty of room on the walls for
failures as well as for successes. Both are retained

AND TRAINING COLLEGES.

within sight of the pupils for a time; and in the hands of a skilful teacher the good and the bad exercises are equally instructive. The wall surface is also available for many other purposes—setting out the work to be done for home lessons; writing out the sums which have to be worked, the lists of words which have to be wrought into sentences; or giving a specimen map or diagram for imitation.

The power of rapid and effective freehand drawing is cultivated more generally, and with more success, among the best American teachers than among our own, and it gives them a great advantage. A diagram sketched out then and there to illustrate a science lesson, a map which grows under the teacher's hand as one fact after another is elicited and explained, have a far greater effect in kindling the interest of children and fixing their attention than any number of engraved or painted pictures, however good. Whatever forms part of the permanent decoration of a schoolroom is apt to be taken for granted, and practically disregarded by children. But a new drawing made *ad hoc* and associated with something which at the time is being enforced or made interesting by the teacher has a value of a far higher kind. The new regulations of our own Science and Art Department respecting the conditions of the drawing certificate for teachers emphasize strongly the importance of uncopied and free blackboard drawing. But the best of the American training colleges have for several years given special attention to this part of the teacher's qualification. I have seen the students of a normal school busily engaged during the midday recess of the juvenile practising school in dashing off with a few simple strokes outline pictures of birds and flowers, of ships or of houses, or copies of the little illustrations to be found in story books; so that when the children returned they should find something new all round the room to look at and to talk about.

It will be seen from the tabulated statement of the requirements in the various grades how large an importance is attached to drawing in the American schools. It is, in fact, the one form of manual training on the value of which all the best educational authorities are agreed. Many misgivings are expressed even by some of the ablest of those authorities about the educational value of other kinds of *Hand-arbeit*, but none as to the importance of drawing and design. In America, as in England, discussions about " technical " and manual instruction excite great public interest. But there are two classes of persons who advocate the introduction of such training into schools; and there is a little confusion between the objects seve- rally aimed at by these two classes. One section of educational authorities desires to train skilled handicraftsmen, and sees with alarm the increasing distaste of the American boy for manual labor. It is said with truth that by far the larger proportion of

Drawing and manual in- struction.

mechanical trades is in the hands of foreigners. This is not altogether surprising. The air of America is full of commercial speculation and enterprise, and of restless ambition. New royal roads to success, new ways of making rapid fortunes, are opening every day. A lad of any promise is attracted to the "store," to the railroad, or the office, and thinks that mechanical labor, if not just a little servile and undignified, is at any rate a very slow process for "getting on" in life. It is believed by many of the advocates of manual training that the best corrective for this growing evil will be the introduction of organized hand-work into the ordinary curriculum of a school; and it is hoped in this way not only to increase the tactual skill of the pupil, but also to awaken an intelligent interest in such work, and to invest it with more dignified associations. Other persons view the whole problem in a different aspect. They believe that, apart from all considerations of industry or utility, the right training of the fingers and the senses is a valuable part of general education, and has an important reflex action on the intelligence of the pupil and on his fitness to perform any of the duties of life. Some very valuable and costly experiments have been tried in many places to meet one or other of these two views. The Technological Institute at Boston, the Pratt Institute at Brooklyn, and the Manual Training School at Chicago have mainly for their purpose to increase the scientific knowledge, the skill and the producing power of those who may look forward to becoming the captains of industry and directors of manufacture. The institutions established by Dr. Felix Adler and Dr. N. Murray Butler in New York, and the Manual Training School at Philadelphia, are types of schools having a more distinctly educational aim. All of these institutions are the product of private munificence, and none of them except the last is incorporated into the public-school system of the city in which it is situated. It is to the energetic initiative of the school superintendent of Philadelphia that the introduction of this new experiment into that city is mainly due. He defends it, not on grounds of any industrial or economic needs, but solely on educational considerations. He says:

"Manual training is founded on the claim that it gives a more complete education than is afforded by the course of instruction now followed in the schools. It undertakes so to modify the existing methods of training as to yield an education that shall make the graduate of the public school a more harmoniously developed and efficient member of society. The instruction given in our schools is too one-sided. . . . To a very large extent the schools neglect the training of those powers which bring the mind into true relations with its physical environment. A very large portion of the time of pupils in schools of every grade is devoted to the study of words. Educational reformers for nearly

AND TRAINING COLLEGES.

300 years have been seeking to remedy this defect. The introduction of object lessons and of science instruction were well-meant efforts in this direction, and manual work is nothing more than a further extension of the same principle. It seeks to train the hand and the eye, not for the purpose of superseding the action of the mind, but as the efficient agents of the mind in gaining a truer and fuller knowledge of the world. Emerson says in his terse way that 'manual labor is the study of the external world.' It is in the spirit of this maxim that the new education seeks to widen the training of children in the direction of the harmonious development of mind and body through such agencies as the best experience may dictate."

It cannot be said that these principles, though accepted by many of the most thoughtful educators in the States, have so far prevailed as to affect the recognized curriculum of school studies in any of the great educational centres. I learned with interest that the School Committee in New York had determined to introduce manual training by way of experiment into nine of their (lower) primary schools and six of the grammar (or upper primary) schools. But on inquiry I found that this meant little more than the adoption for the first time of the little mechanical occupations of the Kindergarten and drawing into the younger classes, and of needlework as a new employment for girls. The *Slojd* or Swedish system of training by woodwork and the use of carpenter's tools is not, so far as I can learn, adopted by any school authority. Drawing, as I have said, is the one manual art about the value of which all are agreed. And, after all, it is the one manual art which is least likely to degenerate into mechanism or to lose its educational character. It is quite conceivable that the arts of carpentering, modelling, sewing, and fashioning paper and metal may, when once acquired, become mere routine, and cease to have any effect on the general development of the learner's capacity and intelligence. But drawing and design are arts capable of infinite developments and applications, and, when once acquired, can never lose their power to stimulate thought, to purify taste, and to call forth new efforts.

An interesting and novel experiment has recently been tried with a view to make the study of drawing more general throughout the States. The "Prang Institute" at Boston has devised a plan for home study and for instruction by correspondence, with a view to meet the needs of teachers in remote places who feel the need of further guidance as to the best mode of teaching. They are furnished with materials, copies, and definite instructions, and their performances in drawing, modelling, and design are sent regularly to headquarters for criticism. Large numbers of teachers have availed themselves of this arrangement, though at a distance from oral in-

AND TRAINING COLLEGES. 43

structors, and are pursuing regular courses of exercise under guidance. I have seen many of the exercises produced under these conditions, and am assured that many of them show unusual excellence. The following programme shows one of the courses prescribed:

"Study of models, and clay modelling of models and objects.

" Laying of plane geometric forms with tablets and sticks to represent objects and ornament.

"Paper cutting and folding.

" *Freehand Drawing:* Pencil holding; free movement ; character of line ; drawing from objects, from dictation, from memory, and from tablet and stick arrangements.

" Making models and objects in paper, cloth, leather, wood, etc.

" Management of the different kinds of work in classes.

"*Constructive Drawing:* Facts of form ; various geometric views or orthographic projections; foreshortening ; conventions ; working drawings ; use of instruments ; drawing to scale ; freehand and instrumental geometric views or orthographic projections of simple models and objects placed in a variety of positions ; geometric problems ; constructive design.

" *Representative Drawing:* Objects as they appear ; foreshortening ; freehand perspective of cylindrical and rectangular solids ; group-

44   NOTES ON AMERICAN SCHOOLS

ing of objects ; composition or pictorial design.

"*Decorative Drawing :* Geometric forms in ornament ; principles in arrangement of forms for decoration ; beauty in ornament ; historic examples of ornament ; natural forms in ornament; conventionalization; decorative design; historic styles of ornament.

"Suggestions for the use of color.

"Collateral reading. Application of drawing in other studies. Why form study and drawing should be taught in public schools.

"The work is arranged in twenty stages, so that students during the course may send their work to Boston twenty times and receive criticisms upon it.

"At the completion of the lessons an examination is given on the work of the course ; and all students passing this examination receive certificates of having passed in the subjects of drawing necessary for teaching the study in grammar schools."

Infant schools, in the English sense of the word,
Infant schools.   are almost unknown in America, chiefly because the course of primary instruction is not generally supposed to begin till the seventh year. In Boston, however, "kindergarten" schools were established, in the first instance, by the private efforts of a benevolent lady, and have since been taken over and incorporated into the public-

school system. In St. Louis also the system of Fröbel was introduced as a voluntary experiment and afterward adopted by the board. In both cases, however, the "kindergarten" was regarded at first as a thing apart from the ordinary primary school. The system and methods were wholly unlike, and the games and manual employments of Fröbel constituted almost the whole occupation of the children. Some disappointment was experienced at the result by many teachers. It was found that this playful discipline did not afford the best preparation for the serious work of the ordinary primary school. The English ideal of an infant school—one in which elementary instruction in reading, writing, and counting is interspersed with simple lessons on the phenomena of nature and of common life, and with interesting and varied manual employments, has not prevailed in America. I confess I greatly prefer it. It seems to me to put what is commonly called "kindergarten" methods and discipline into their proper place, rather as organic parts of a good and rounded system of juvenile training, as helps to the general development of the observant faculty and to the acquisition of knowledge, than as constituting even in the earliest years a separate organization, having aims and principles different from those which should prevail during the rest of the school life. Whatever is good and true in the principles of Fröbel and Rousseau, is applicable not to infants only, but also to the discipline of children of all ages. Separate Fröbelian institutions, for "kindergarten" training and manual employments alone, are in my opinion foredoomed to failure.

I did not think either the reading or the writing of the scholars whose performances I witnessed were better, age for age, than those which one meets with every day in good elementary schools at home. Less use is made in the lower classes of large hand as a means of showing the true forms and proportions of letters, and as a general rule the style of writing appropriate to small-hand is adopted from the first. The use of the type-writer is now so much more common in American houses of business than in England that I had few opportunities of seeing the handwriting of the youths who had gone from school into such houses; but what I saw has not been clearer or more readable than that of lads of the same age in London. The reading books as a rule are bright, well illustrated, and attractive; but rather more fragmentary than our own, and are generally designed rather to form a taste for reading than to convey much information. I was very glad to find that the absurd practice so common in English schools of constantly interrupting the reading lesson for exercises in oral spelling was everywhere discouraged in America. Spelling is a matter for the visual memory and for transcription, not for oral recitation. *Pictures* of words need to be seen and recognized, and time is terribly wasted by the mere utterance of the letters

AND TRAINING COLLEGES.

that compose them. The following passage from the "manual" issued by one of the city school superintendents deserves the attention of English as well as American teachers :

"Do not use concert drill. The impression made upon the mind by writing the same word often and by frequent reviews in the form of dictation will be found much better aids to the memory than any amount of oral repetition. It is next to impossible to prevent concert exercises in spelling from degenerating into a mere unconscious utterance of words, a species of action destructive of every purpose for which a well-ordered school is maintained."

One exercise in reading I found in the grammar schools of America which might be usefully adopted here. Scholars are set down for a quarter of an hour to read a page or two in silence, and are told that at the end of the time there will be questions and conversation upon it. We often act as if the only reading to be performed in school was reading aloud in class. Thus the habit of using a book in the one way in which its use will be of most value to a scholar in after life—reading to himself and feeling himself responsible for getting at and appropriating its meaning—is not properly acquired.

Much more attention is paid than in our schools to what I may call "oral composition," Oral composition.
to exercises in which the scholar is called upon to stand up and reproduce a story, or to say

what he knows or what he thinks about the subject. *E. g.*, a list of words which have occurred during a reading lesson is written on the board, and the scholars are called on individually to rise and make sentences, containing one or more of the words. A rough outline picture is drawn, and the scholar is asked to make a little story about it. Answers to questions are expected to be given in whole sentences, not in single words. Time is reserved at the end of the lesson for recapitulating parts of it by the scholars themselves, with less of prompting and questioning than is common in our schools. Often a boy or girl is called on to come forward and catechise the class on what has been learned. No doubt this causes delay, and makes a lesson seem to move slowly and to cover but little ground ; but the principle underlying the practice is entirely right. There is no true teaching unless the learner is made to speak his own words, as well as to listen to those of an instructor.

> " Minds that have nothing to confer
> Find little to perceive."

This is not unfrequently overlooked. The opposite practice, which I have often to complain of at home, has the disadvantage of giving the learners too little to do for themselves. The teacher often hurries on, asking questions which admit of being answered in single words ; satisfied if he secures interest and attention and if the scholars seem to acquiesce in what

AND TRAINING COLLEGES. 49

he states. But he needs to be reminded that ac-
quiescence is not knowledge ; that it is very possible to assent to many propositions without understanding them ; and that Charles Kingsley's playful
description of a school in which "the master learned
all the lessons and the scholars heard them" is not
wholly a figment of a novelist's imagination.

The great facility possessed by the average American in the art of public speaking is not   Elocution.
only fostered by the numerous conven-
tions and ceremonials which form so conspicuous
a feature of transatlantic life, it is largely encouraged by the discipline of the schools. Children are
practised from the first in looking large numbers of
other children in the face and reciting with courage
and self-possession. English readers of American
books, must, however, be on their guard against
misunderstanding the word "recitation," which so
frequently occurs in them. It does not mean, as
with us, an elocutionary effort of any kind ; but it
simply denotes any oral lesson or catechetical exercise. Nevertheless, recitation in our sense of the
word is practised in various forms. If the scholars
have prepared a written exercise they are asked to
read it aloud to the class. Solos are to be heard as
well as choruses in the music lessons. The teacher
will often write or select from a book a little dia-
logue, which is learned by three or four picked
scholars, and recited in the hearing of the class with
much dramatic action and emphasis. Connected

with every school and college, from the primary school up to Harvard University, there is an annual ceremonial day, on which, in the hearing of parents and the public, the pupils who have written the best essays or who can do anything particularly well, are called on to declaim or otherwise display their powers. It is needless to say that these exhibitions are very popular, that they keep up a sense of pride and local interest in the public schools, and that they powerfully stimulate the more ambitious scholars. That they also encourage self-consciousness and the love of display, that the show compositions are often not original productions, and that there was a slight air of unreality and pretentiousness about some of the " commencement " exercises which I witnessed, must, I fear, be admitted. This drawback is fully recognized by many of the best teachers with whom I conversed on the subject, but when due precautions are taken I cannot doubt that there is a genuine advantage in these displays, both as means of enlisting popular and parental sympathy in the work of education and as an incentive to scholars to do their best.

It seemed to me that an undue proportion of what was learned was learned by heart,

Memory exercise. and that even the oral exercises which were supposed to be spontaneous were too much alike, and conformed too often to certain conventional patterns which were in constant use in the schools. What is oddly called "memorizing" is a

AND TRAINING COLLEGES.

very favorite exercise; but it is often confined to the reproduction of scraps of information or short passages from text-books. Many more rules, definitions, and aphorisms are committed to memory in American than in English schools. I heard in one class the boys get up one after another and give by rote in succession a few sentences recording the names, dates, and chief performances of the eighteen presidents of the United States. In another school, the girls recited in order the names of principal inventors and discoverers, with a description of the exploits of each. Of course, all these facts are worth knowing, but the particular words in which the compiler of the text-book has embodied them have no value in themselves; and as far as they have any effect at all, learning them by rote tends to discourage any effort of thought about the subject itself. I am glad to know that in England the only purely *memoriter* exercise prescribed in the Code is the learning of good poetry, in which not only the substance is interesting, but the form is itself valuable, and has a grace and charm and therefore an educative value of its own. The practice so common in our best schools at home of learning by heart in the highest classes one hundred of the noblest lines of a play like *Julius Cæsar*, and reading in connection with the whole drama some of the history of the period, is very little followed in the American schools. In many of them a great deal of what is learned by heart has no literary merit, and can therefore do little to improve the vocabulary or to refine the taste of the learner.

The teaching of arithmetic is greatly helped in America by the fortunate circumstances that all the money is decimal, and that a good many of the antiquated terms found in English tables of weights and measures are not in use. Hence all compound arithmetic is easier, and time is saved which can be well devoted to the explanation of principles and to examination of the properties of numbers, and the reasons for arithmetical processes. In most of the schemes of instruction the arithmetical course is laid out in a careful and logical order; the method of Grube being very generally adopted. The characteristic feature of this method is that it does not regard addition, subtraction, multiplication, and division as four processes graduated in difficulty, and to be learned in succession ; but it assumes that the true progression is from small numbers to large. Hence the beginner takes, for example, the number twelve. He is made to see and to count cubes, balls, or other objects. He adds, subtracts, multiplies, and divides all the numbers up to twelve. He is shown or helped to find out in how many ways that number is made up of parts. He learns all its fractions and aliquot parts ; he applies the number to hours, to money, and to inches, and whatever arithmetical process is possible within that narrow limit he

Arithmetic.

AND TRAINING COLLEGES. 53

learns to perform. After that he proceeds in the next class, say, as far as the number 50, and will take up the arithmetic of one dollar, not going beyond the limit, but performing every operation within it. Big numbers and elaborate notation are reserved till later. It is believed that by knowing all the properties of small and manageable numbers, and by varying the exercises upon them, the scholar obtains a far better mastery over figures, and a truer preparation for dealing with more complex magnitudes, than if he works in succession a number of sums in groups, each group illustrating a single rule. The method seems to me a good and rational one, and I was much pleased with the results. It is certainly more interesting to the children. The helpless way in which scholars at home sometimes ask, when a question is given, " What rule is it in ? " is a sure proof that they have been unintelligently taught.

Much use is made of mental arithmetic in all the schools, and the " manuals " suggest some ingenious devices for varying the form of the questions. Here, for example, is a little artifice which I found in very effective use in some of the lower classes. The nine digits are written on the board in a circle, and in any irregular order. The teacher takes a pointer and begins, for example, with an outside number, 4. He points in rapid

Mental arithmetic.

succession to each of the numbers, requiring the pupils to say as he goes round from the figure 3 to the right, 4, 7, 12, 20, 27, 31, 37, 39, 40, 49. He then begins again from the top, or from any one number in the circle, and moves round to the left. By trying at different points, starting with different numbers from without, he may get an endless variety of combinations, and make the addition of any one number to another unit very familiar. And whenever he sees that there is a hitch or pause in proceeding from one number to another, he notes that particular combination as one in which mistakes are more likely to occur, and gives a number of special exercises upon it.

One excellent practice is in general use in the best American schools which I have seen. A scholar is frequently asked to make sums, to set a question in a rule, and to come forward and work it out in the presence of the class. Sometimes, when a process has been explained, the home lesson does not take the form of set exercises to be wrought out; but the scholars are told to invent for themselves, and work by next day any sums they like in illustration of the rule. On the whole, it does not seem to me that the boys and girls are working questions quite so difficult as those of the same age in England, or that their answers are more generally correct. Ability to manipulate numbers is understood to come earlier than power to comprehend mathematical demonstration, and

AND TRAINING COLLEGES.

such demonstration is often deferred. But, speaking generally, the rationale of the rules is often better explained than at home. It should be observed that in the exercises for solution much care is taken to give practical problems such as would occur in ordinary business—writing out bills, commercial letters, calculations of bank interest, and fictitious ledgers and cash-books.

All the schemes of instruction insist in some form on object lessons, or "observation lessons," as they are often called. In some cases hygiene is the favorite subject, in others botany, in some natural history, in others the ordinary scenes and incidents of town or country life. Grammar and analysis are included in all cases; but in the earlier classes the English exercises consist mainly of simple composition and punctuation, and the use of capitals; formal grammar being deferred a little later than in English schools. The logical analysis and synthesis of sentences receive a good deal of attention. But verbal analysis, the structure and decomposition of words, the meaning of significant prefixes and final syllables, and the grouping together of words having a common root, or a common element in meaning—an exercise which in judicious hands is found so stimulating in many English schools—is not always prescribed or practised. I could observe little practical difference between American schools and our own in regard to the

Object or "observation lessons," etc.

teaching of geography and history. The maps were often excellent and well finished, but not better than are to be seen any day in London Board schools ; and our own method of beginning with the geography of the immediate neighborhood, and connecting from the first physical geography with commercial and political facts, is generally adopted. If the scholars showed, as a rule, a fuller acquaintance with the history of their own country than English children of the same age, it may be accounted for by the fact that there is much less of it to learn. Few of the prescribed lessons go back even to the colonial days. It is to the glorious annals of American progress during the century succeeding the Revolution that the attention of the scholars is chiefly directed.

Closely connected with this subject, another feature of American schools deserves particular mention. Special lessons are everywhere given on the American Constitution, on the rights and duties of American citizens, of the President, of Congress, of the Senate, and of the States. National anniversaries are very religiously observed. "On the school days immediately preceding the 4th of July and the 22d of February (Washington's birthday) in each year," say the regulations of the New York School Board, "the principals of all the grammar schools in the city shall assemble the pupils of their respective schools and read, or cause to be read, to them either the

Lessons in patriotism.

AND TRAINING COLLEGES.

'Declaration of Independence' or 'Washington's farewell address to the people of the United States,' combining therewith such other patriotic exercises as may be advisable." There can be no doubt that in this and other ways, the schools try successfully, not only to inform the children about the government under which they live, but to inspire them with a pride in their country and its institutions. An American boy thinks that in no other country would it be possible for him to enjoy real freedom, or so many civic privileges. I was talking to a class once about the meanings of some words which were written on the board as a verbal exercise, and "equality" being one of the words, I asked the boys to put it into a sentence. One after another made up a sentence about the equality of all American citizens, and when the question was further put, "Equality in what?—in height, in size, in fortune, in good looks, in wisdom, in goodness?" the negative answers were followed unanimously by the phrase, "in political rights." It was evidently the feeling of the class that such equality in political rights existed nowhere else in the world. One may be amused at this, but it is nevertheless true, on both sides of the Atlantic, that a boy is more likely hereafter to do something to make his country proud of him, if he is early taught to be proud of his country, and to have some good reason for being proud of it.

In the country places, throughout the States of

58 NOTES ON AMERICAN SCHOOLS

the Union and the provinces of the Canadian
Dominion, it is a common practice to
set apart one day in April, May, or
June for planting trees, shrubs, and flowers in the
school precincts, and for the general ornamentation of the school premises. The authorities per-
mit this to count as a lawful school day. During
the forenoon the grounds are levelled, stones and
refuse removed, holes made for the trees, a flower-
bed is laid out or a part of the ground is sodded or
seeded with lawn grass. While the boys are thus
engaged, the girls are employed in putting in order
and ornamenting the schoolroom, arranging flowers, and displaying specimens of maps, writing, and
other manual work. Trees planted are associated
with the name of a class or a teacher, or of some
public event.

Arbor day.

One could not help being impressed everywhere
by the excellence of the discipline, and
the more so as it is said to be maintained almost uniformly without resorting to cor-
poral punishment. Indeed, in most of the State
and city regulations teachers are absolutely forbid-
den to inflict such punishment at all. There was
no lack of evidence of high animal spirits outside
the schools ; but within there seemed to be little
difficulty in maintaining discipline. Even at the
universities, at Columbia and at Harvard, where I
witnessed both the out-door sports and the academic
ceremonial, I was struck by the dignity and serious-

Discipline.

AND TRAINING COLLEGES.

ness of the students in the college itself, the absence, not merely of rowdyism, but of all unseemly shouting or unruliness.

The chief feature in the schemes of instruction is the minuteness with which all the *General character of the* details are specified and the little room *schemes of* that is left for the discretion or special *instruction.* preferences of the teacher. In the high schools and universities the practice of prescribing "elective" subjects is very common; but here the choice is open to the parent or scholar, not to the teacher. In the schemes for primary and grammar schools, corresponding to our public elementary schools at home, there are hardly ever any alternative or optional subjects. There is a fixed *menu,* and not, as in the English schedules, provision for a *diner à la carte* in the form of a list of class-subjects, or specific subject from which the teacher may choose that which he can teach best, and which is most useful or most appreciated in his own district. Every subject is obligatory. The books to be used, the limits of work to be done in each grade or standard, are, in most cases, rigidly prescribed. I was looking at the copy-books in one school and observed that the series of exercises was graduated on a novel and rather elaborate theory, beginning with an analysis of the parts of letters. I asked the teacher whether she found the plan worked well. She replied that it worked ill and that she greatly disliked it; but, she added, "these copy-

60 NOTES ON AMERICAN SCHOOLS

books are prescribed by the school superintendent and we must not use any other." Repeatedly I have been told, when asking some simple question closely connected with the subject in hand, that it was "beyond the grade." A class of boys of 13 was working fractions, and when I was questioning them on a fraction and suggesting that other figures similarly related would express the same fraction, I happened to use the word "proportion." The teacher stopped me at once with the remark that proportion did not come until the next grade. There is certainly less room for spontaneity or originality of plan on the part of the teacher than in our own country. It seemed to me, too, that many of the authorized time-tables cut up the day's work into too many short lessons on different subjects, and that the teaching was often scrappy and superficial, affording less room for the thorough examination of a subject than might be desired. Text-books and certain accepted formulas appeared to dominate the work of the classes too much, and, in spite of the undoubted merits of some features of the educational system, I have not the least reason to believe that American boys and girls are more soundly taught or are provided with a better intellectual outfit for the business and duties of life than English children of the same age, who are brought up in a good elementary school.

The chief executive officer and the adviser of the local educational authority is the School Superin-

AND TRAINING COLLEGES.

tendent. He occupies a position wholly unlike that of any scholastic officer in any country in Europe. Within his own domain, whether a State, a county, or a city, he combines in himself the characters of a minister of public instruction, an inspector of schools, a licenser of teachers, and a professor of pedagogy. Under the sanction of his board or committee he draws up the detailed regulations for the work of all classes in the schools, and often appends to them a manual, or at least an explanatory memorandum prescribing the method in which each subject shall be taught. He conducts, with the assistance of his staff of inspectors, the periodical exam- *His duties.* inations for determining the list of promotions among scholars from grade to grade. He sets the questions. He examines all candidates for the office of teacher in his district, and awards to them diplomas authorizing their employment in schools, and stating the grades of teaching for which they are severally qualified. It is part of his duty to hold "institutes" or assemblies of teachers, and to instruct those of them who have not been previously trained in the work of their special classes. He often conducts voluntary periodical conferences with the older teachers, and gives lectures to them on the history and philosophy of education. He is assisted by a staff of inspectors or supervisors who visit schools under his direction and share with him the duty of examining children for promotion.

The school superintendent.

Sometimes he has an ingenious plan for availing himself of the services of the teachers in the annual examinations. He arranges that each question shall be answered on a separate sheet of paper, and then confides the marking of all the answers to one given question to one person. In this way he secures uniformity of judgment and avoids all suspicion of partiality. At his central bureau are often to be found a good professional library, for lending and reference, for the use of teachers ; specimen juvenile libraries suited to different classes of schools, and a museum of objects and appliances illustrative of the best methods of teaching. One of the ablest of the school superintendents showed me some large portfolios and bound volumes in which he had carefully collected and dated during some years past the best specimens of work done at the annual examinations, drawings, written answers to questions, themes, compositions, and the like. He was thus able, he said, to compare the work of one year with another, and to form an exact estimate of general progress or of the working of any new experiment.

The person charged with these multifarious and

His qualifications.

important duties has almost invariably —I never met with one exception to the rule—been himself a teacher. Not, indeed, an *elementary* teacher, for if he were it is urged with some truth he would not be so likely to secure the confidence and respect of those whom he superintended, and would not be qualified either to examine high schools or to advise the board in reference to the due co-ordination of the work of primary and secondary instruction. But he has nearly always before his appointment served with distinction as master in a high school, or as professor in a normal or other college. He is, therefore, familiar with all the details of school work, and able to give valuable counsel in regard to methods. To this fact he owes much of his influence among teachers and much of his public usefulness. If to the same fact he also owes certain prepossessions, and a certain lack of intellectual detachment, which render it difficult for him to recognize impartially the merit of good work of very different types, it must be admitted that these are possible disadvantages. But, in the opinion of the best authorities, they are enormously outweighed by the advantages which he has derived from his previous educational experience.

The main drawback to the usefulness of the school superintendent is the precarious tenure of his office. He is appointed by a local school committee, which is itself directly or indirectly the product of popular election, and which is liable to frequent changes. He is himself subject to triennial, or even to annual, re-election, and cannot count on that re-election unless he is *persona grata* to the local authority of the day. He is entitled to no pension and to no compensation for loss of office. He is, it is true, not one of that large army of functionaries whose offices become vacant on the accession of a new president, for he is not an officer of the Federal Government, but of the State or the city. Local politics, however, are subject to fluctuations certainly not less frequent and decisive than those of the Union itself. Every school superintendent has, therefore, a personal interest in local elections, which sometimes necessarily identifies him with party controversies, and which must, in any case, tend to withdraw his attention from his proper duties. Moreover, he has a strong motive to ingratiate himself with those who will have the power to re-elect him. The exercise of patronage is the pleasantest and often the most coveted part of the prerogative of a local alderman or committeeman. He wishes, it may be, to procure for a niece or other *protégée* an appointment as teacher. Her qualifications may not be high, but the *fiat* of the school superintendent will entitle her to a diploma, and that officer is under the strongest temptation to grant it on lenient terms. This is not the place in which to dwell upon the large question of Civil Service Reform, which is so anxiously discussed by American statesmen, but within the sphere of educational work the need for it is no less felt than in the Customs or in the Post Office. A body of public officers like the members of the permanent Civil Service in England, bound by the traditional etiquette of their profession to hold themselves aloof from all party politics, and to place their best services at the disposal of chiefs of differ-

AND TRAINING COLLEGES.

ent administrations, yet, at the same time, secure in their position *quamdiu se bene gesserint,* does not exist in America. Till it exists the nation will not induce the ablest men to take up departmental duty as a life's profession, nor will it obtain even from those who now undertake it the fullest and highest service which they are capable of rendering.

Practically inseparable from the American system, there is another danger, on which definite statements could not be properly made without great caution, even were the data for accurate generalization less obscure and more accessible than they are. The school authorities in their official programmes prescribe not only subjects of instruction, but also, in most cases, the books and the apparatus which should be employed. Occasionally, but not frequently, there is an authorized list of books from which the teachers are under certain conditions free to choose. More often the list of school-books is definitely enforced. Large pecuniary interests—those of publishers and producers of school appliances—are therefore involved. The smartness and energy of American traders are well known, and since the introduction of a new series of copybooks or of a manual may bring a large profit to a business house it is not surprising that the way is open to a good deal of subterranean influence if not to actual bribery. It is known that some great publishing firms spend considerable sums in manipulating the elections for school committees, with a special view to the adoption of particular reading-books or text-books. A great temptation is therefore presented to those officers who are charged with the duty of framing the lists of school requisites, and experience shows that this temptation is not always resisted.

This difficulty is partly, though not wholly, avoided by the practice which is adopted in the Province of Ontario. Here, when the Minister of Public Instruction approves a reading-book or text-book, the Education Department buys up the copyright, and thus becomes a distributor, without any intermediary agent, of its own books. This plan makes it next to impossible that any officer of the department should have a private commercial understanding with a publisher. But it does not overcome the graver difficulty. The selected book, however good, will certainly not be in the judgment of *all* the best teachers the fittest book for their own purpose, nor that which they can use the most effectively. And even though it may be, on the whole, the best book which could be chosen, the fact that its use has been enforced by authority tends to discourage the most valuable forms of educational enterprise, and to make the production of a still better book difficult.

The subject of school superintendence connects Inspection and itself closely with the whole question examination. of inspection and examination, and with the means adopted in order to secure the continued

AND TRAINING COLLEGES.

efficiency of the schools. A comparison of these means with those employed in our own country might prove misleading, inasmuch as the conditions are wholly dissimilar. There is nothing in America analogous to the Education Department in England, distributing from a central office a vast sum annually voted by Parliament in aid of local effort, and at the same time leaving all initiative—the choice of teachers, of books, and of methods, and the whole of the organization and daily discipline—to independent local bodies. The boards and committees of an American county or city are themselves the school managers ; they appoint, pay, and dismiss teachers and prescribe plans and machinery, and their income is derived from one source only—the public fund, placed at their disposal by the taxpayers. They have in their hands many means of keeping up the standard of the schools, while the central government in England has but one—the power to grant or withhold subsidies, and to proportion the amount of those subsidies to the proved efficiency of the teaching. The method generally adopted by the various school authorities in America is to issue a very definite programme, to prescribe minutely the work to be done in each "grade" or class, to put forth also a manual or explanatory memorandum indicating the methods which are to be adopted in teaching each subject ; and then, by means of frequent inspection, to find out whether these directions are habitually carried

68 NOTES ON AMERICAN SCHOOLS

into effect. There are examinations, of course, especially when once a year the scholars are individually tested in order to determine whether they are qualified for promotion; but the main purpose of inspection is to ascertain whether the teachers are using the approved methods and conforming to the official programme. This plan of inspection has some obvious merits; but it is open to many objections, and is deeply disliked by many of the best teachers. In England, if the universities examine the public schools, if external examining authorities make an annual report upon a grammar school or a girls' high school, or if H. M. inspectors examine an elementary school, it is with the *results* of the work that they are concerned. The methods, the books, and the organization are left to the discretion of the teachers, who, whether engaged in higher or lower schools, would regard as an intolerable restraint the authority of any external body which laid down for the daily work of each class regulations as minute as those contained in some of the American manuals. Such regulations, though they are often drawn with great ability, and though they are of undoubted value to inexperienced or unskilful teachers, have a tendency to discourage originality, to destroy all sense of freedom and elbow-room on the part of the best teachers, and to make school work run in too mechanical a routine. While I was in New York an indignation meeting was held, and attended by many

AND TRAINING COLLEGES.

teachers and friends of education, to protest against the existing system, to set up a society for the reform of the city schools, and to denounce the " hated manuals " put forth by the board. Very strong language was used at the meeting and in the press. " Our system," it was said, " does not properly educate, and is conducted too much on the principle that the teacher's work is to cram the pupil with hard facts. The school system of this city is nothing more or less than a magnificent piece of machinery, crushing out, whether designedly or not, all individuality. Uniformity is the thing aimed at, and the uniformity achieved is that of mediocrity." I thought I had heard language of this kind somewhat nearer home, but I had never before heard it used against public authorities because they did *not* measure the teaching in schools by its results, but would insist on minute and mechanical rules controlling the processes by which the results were produced. And over and over again I have been asked by teachers what sort of test was applied to educational work in England; and when I have replied that it was the business of officials here to ascertain what work had been done, but not to criticise methods, except in so far as those methods were shown to have failed to achieve their purpose, teachers have invariably told me that they would greatly prefer being judged under such a system, and that it would be far more tolerable and effective than their own. The truth is that till the end of time any conceivable system which subjects either teaching work or any other work to external criticism is sure to be unsatisfactory to some of those who are criticised. But once admit that public authority is to be brought to bear on school work at all, there are, it would seem, only two possible ways of doing it. Whether the immediate object be to award credit to the teachers, or to assess the share of a public fund to which the school should be entitled, or to make a report for the information of the public, is immaterial. The work of a school must be estimated either by its methods and machinery or by its results; and of the two the former plan hampers teachers and restricts their freedom far more than the latter. It presupposes that the method approved by authority is the best in all circumstances and in the hands of all teachers; and it greatly discourages all independent effort and all invention of new and better methods.

I may add here that the salaries of school super-

Salaries of school superintendents.

intendents vary greatly according to the size and wealth of the communities which they serve. The highest salary enjoyed by any city superintendent I know is $8,000, the lowest $2,500. County superintendents, as a rule, receive less. In Delaware, for example, the salary of a county superintendent is fixed at $1,000. Generally the stipend of a superintendent is fixed so as slightly to exceed the largest salary enjoyed by the

AND TRAINING COLLEGES. 71

teacher of the most important school which is under the supervision of the board. The average salaries, of the inspectors who serve under the superintendent are also somewhat higher than those of the teachers. and range from $800 to $2,000.

The number of teachers employed in all the public schools and colleges of the States is given, for 1887, as 104,249 men and 191,439 women. When it is considered that this number includes all the teachers and professors in high schools and many State colleges, and that men form the majority of the teachers in the southern States and in Indiana, the preponderance of female teachers in the northern and eastern States is seen to be very large. As a rule, all the work of the primary departments and nearly all that of the grammar schools is performed by women. The chief exception to this rule is that there is often a head or presiding master over the whole of a grammar department, and he not infrequently has one or two masters to assist him in the higher classes. Although, theoretically, the schools are mixed, boys and girls often going to the same school, there is generally a division of the boys' and girls' classes in the higher grades whenever the number of pupils is large enough to admit of such a division. There being no system of pupil-teachership, candidates enter the profession at 17 or 18, having generally passed through a high school, and subsequently satisfied the school superintendent by passing an examination. No class prejudices prevent the daughters of lawyers or clergymen from undertaking the office of teacher in a primary or grammar school; and, as a rule, the teachers in such schools are of rather higher social rank, and have often had a wider general education, than those employed in English elementary schools. They are, in the first instance, after probation, licensed only to take charge of a class of a given grade, generally the lowest; and if they desire a diploma qualifying them to take charge of a higher class, they must come up again for further examination, and have their fitness to take such a class duly certified. This practice appears *prima facie* to have two disadvantages. It puts the least experienced and skilful teachers to the lowest classes. where experience and skill are often most needed. It attaches each teacher too closely to a particular class, and cuts up the whole school into practically independent parts. The system lacks the elasticity which would allow of the free use of an assistant for that particular work which she could do best, and it fails to give to the members of the staff a due sense of responsibility for the efficiency and repute of the school as a whole. Marriage is generally held to be an act of resignation, and, in fact, the average tenure of office on the part of the female teachers does not much exceed three years. In the single State of New York there are 31,726 teachers in the public

AND TRAINING COLLEGES. 73

schools, of whom 7,000 entered on their work in the year 1887, but this number includes all the masters of high schools and male professors in colleges, most of whom remain much longer in the profession than women. Even these men, however, more often adopt teaching as a temporary employment, and leave it for the ministry, for the newspaper press, or for commerce, than the corresponding class of men in this country.

The salaries of teachers differ greatly in different places. The city of New York Their salaries. may be quoted as having made an exceptionally liberal provision in this respect. Principals of the larger grammar schools receive from $2,250 to $3,000, vice-principals from $1,800 to $2,000; and in the smaller grammar schools principals are paid from $1,200 to $1,700, and vice-principals $1,000 to $1,200. The salaries of male assistants range from $1,000 to $2,000, and of female assistants from $500 to $1,100. They are graduated partly by length of service, but principally by the grade or class which is placed in the hands of the teacher. Promotion generally means taking an advanced class. In the country places the chief teacher sometimes receives from $900 to $1,200, and his or her assistants $400 to $500. The average salaries of white teachers, however, in the State of Maryland, scarcely reach $300. The engagement of country teachers is often by the month only, and even by the week. In New

Hampshire the average wages of male teachers were $41, and of female teachers $24 per month; and in Pennsylvania men received on an average $38.50 and women $20.80 per month. They who would compare these salaries with those of English teachers must bear in mind the higher rents and greater cost of living, and will find it safe to divide by *six* rather than by five, in order to represent the purchasing power of these stipends in English sovereigns.

Their qualifications.

There is no general standard of qualification recognized in the States. Each school committee has its own regulations, and insists that a teacher shall satisfy the requirements of its own superintendent; and the diploma given in one State, even to a graduate of a normal school, is not available in any other State, and, indeed, is very rarely accepted without further examination. A certificate of professional competency is, therefore, wholly local in its application. Considering the very short time which the average teacher spends in the profession, it is not surprising that comparatively few give up the needful time and effort to obtain special preparation in normal schools. The proportion of trained to untrained teachers is highest—56 per cent.—in Massachusetts; it varies from 20 to 26 per cent. in Vermont, Rhode Island, Pennsylvania, and California. It is lowest in the State of New York, 4 per cent. But of the whole number of public teachers employed in the States it

AND TRAINING COLLEGES. 75

is computed that no more than 10 per cent. have received any normal training at all; and "normal training," it must be remembered, is very differently interpreted, meaning often twelve months', six months', or even three months' attendance at a training college.

The normal or training colleges are very unequally distributed through the coun- Training colleges. In some of the Southern and Western States—notably in Colorado, Delaware, Ohio, Georgia, Kentucky, Mississippi, South Carolina—there are no normal schools, at least, none available for white teachers. In Pennsylvania, however, there are 11 normal schools, in Massachusetts 6, in Maine 4, in California 2, in Alabama 6—3 for white and 3 for colored students —in Connecticut 4, and in New York 9. Many of these institutions, however, are not purely normal schools, in the English sense of the word. The largest of them all—for example, that in New York city—is a high school with 1,600 pupils, and its course of instruction lasts four years. The first and second of these years, and a large part of the third, are devoted to ordinary academic instruction; and it is in the third and fourth years only that the professional training of future teachers is undertaken. Since large numbers of the pupils quit the institution at the end of the second and third years, and have had no intention of taking up the teaching profession, it is only the comparatively small number who "graduate" by completing the four years' course that can be said to be actually trained as teachers; and all of these find employment in the city as primary, grammar, or high school teachers. Many other of the normal schools are in like manner ordinary high schools, with a class of advanced pupils in the last year, or in the last six months, studying school methods and organization. The theory of teaching is one of the "elective studies" in some of the local high schools. As a rule, the purely normal colleges are for women only, but in several of them a very small number, not exceeding 10 per cent., of male students may be found. The colleges are nearly always day schools, the students living at home or in lodgings. Men who intend to devote themselves to the teaching profession prefer to graduate at one of the ordinary higher colleges, and to rely on their academic distinctions; and do not, except to a very inconsiderable extent, go to normal institutions. Several of the universities and colleges have, however, contrived to engraft a teaching or pedagogic faculty upon the ordinary academic organization. The University of Michigan, at Ann Arbor, was one of the first to try this experiment. Mr. W. H. Payne, one of the leading writers on education in America, was charged with the duty of initiating the work, and in his hands it has had considerable success. Many of the young men and women in the university were found to be destined for important educational posts, as high school principals and lecturers, and as superintendents of city schools, and a course of special training was devised for them in the history, science, and art of teaching. But these students are not separated from the rest in the general studies, and it is regarded as a great advantage that no such separation is made. The branch of "pedagogics" is supplementary, and forms one of the "elective" courses which the university permits to count for a degree. In several of the western universities the same experiment is being tried with some success ; but at Baltimore, at the College of the City of New York, at Columbia University, and at the great college for ladies at Wellesley, although experiments have been made in establishing chairs of education, the number of students availing themselves of the privilege has been comparatively small. There is in America, as in England, a growing conviction that special training and a knowledge of the principles of teaching are as much needed by teachers in higher and secondary schools as by those who teach the rudiments, but it cannot be said that effect is given to this conviction on any large scale.

The character of the instruction in the training college proper will be readily inferred from the following programme, which is, with small exceptions, common to all the State normal schools of Massachusetts :

78   NOTES ON AMERICAN SCHOOLS

" The design of the normal school is strictly pro-
Scheme of nor- *fessional ;* that is, to prepare, in the
mal instruc-
tion.   best possible manner, the students for
the work of organizing, governing, and teaching
the public schools of the commonwealth.

"To this there must be added the most thorough
knowledge of the branches of learning to be taught
in the schools, of the best method of teaching those
branches, and of right mental training.

"*The two years' course includes the following
studies:*

Geometry, arithmetic, algebra, bookkeeping.

Physics, chemistry, mineralogy, botany, zool-
ogy, physiology, geography, geology, astron-
omy.

Reading, orthography, etymology, grammar,
rhetoric, literature, composition.

Penmanship, drawing, vocal music, gymnastics,
military drill.

Psychology, science and art of education, school
organization, history of education.

History, civil polity of Massachusetts and of the
United States, and school laws of Massachusetts.

"*The four years' course, in addition to the
studies named above, includes:*

Advanced algebra and geometry, trigonometry
and surveying.

Advanced physics, chemistry, and botany.

General history, drawing, English literature.

AND TRAINING COLLEGES.

Latin and French required ; Greek and German,
as the principal and visitors of the school
shall decide.

" The nature of the purely professional part of
this course will be best understood by the help of
the following detailed syllabus :

" *Education.* — The educational study of man.
1. The study of the human body for the laws of
physical health, strength, and beauty as conditions
for the activity of the mind. 2. The study of
educational psychology. Definition and division of
psychology. The intellect—reason, the presentative, representative, and reflective powers. The
sensibilities—the appetites, instinct, desires, affec-
tions. The will and the moral nature. The subject is taught from the facts of the student's con-
sciousness. The end sought is the knowledge of
the powers of the mind, the order of their development, the conditions and products of their activity,
and the ability to use this knowledge in the education of children.

" *Science and Art of Teaching.*—Principles of
education, as derived from study of man. The art
of teaching—definitions : knowledge of the mind,
the pupil, the subject ; selection and arrangement
of subject-matter ; method of teaching ; language,
voice, and manner of the teacher; means of making
the teaching impressive ; object and method of
criticism ; teacher's preparation. Course of studies
arranged for the primary, intermediate, and higher

grades; method of teaching in the studies of the primary course and practice with children.

"*School Organization.*—What it is to organize a school. Advantages of a good organization. Opening of the school. Classification of the school. Distribution of studies. Arrangement of the exercises. Provisions relating to order.

"*School Government.*—Definition of government and what government implies in the governor and in the subject. School government; definition, the teacher's right to govern, and the end of school government. The motives to be used in school government, and the method of their application.

"*History of Education.*—School Laws of Massachusetts."

At the Worcester Normal School there is a system of what is called apprenticeship, which, inasmuch as the young people are required by it to do actual service in the schools during the period of their training, is the nearest approach I have met with in America to what is known as pupil-teachership in England. The student of 16 or 17, after three terms, or a year and a half in the normal school, is allowed to go into one of the public schools of the city of Worcester to serve as assistant to the teacher of that school; to take part in the instruction, management, and general work, under the direction of the head master; and even to act as substitute for the class teacher for an hour, a half-day, or a day,

AND TRAINING COLLEGES. 81

at the discretion of the master and with the approval of the superintendent. One student only at a time is assigned to any one teacher; but each student serves in at least three grades of schools in the course of his term of service, the duration of which is six months, or half a school year. After finishing his apprenticeship the student resumes his course at the normal school, spending another half-year there before receiving his diploma.

During the period of apprenticeship four days of each week are devoted exclusively to teaching by those employed in the work. One day of the week (Wednesday) is spent by them in the normal school, where they are employed, not in the ordinary study and work of the institution, but in the following manner:

" They hold such consultation with the teachers of the school, and make such use of books, as may be most helpful to them in their immediate work as apprentices.

"They make informal statements of such facts of their experience as may be of advantage to the other students to hear, concerning ways of teaching, cases of discipline, and the like, keeping in mind always the private character of the daily life of the school-room, and under special warning against revelations that might seem objectionable.

" Each apprentice keeps a diary of the occupation and experience of every day's service, and this record is inspected by the faculty of the normal school. He also makes out a report at the end of his term, in which he gives his own estimate of his success in his work."

Education as a science. It is a characteristic feature of all the best of the American training schools that in them more attention is given than in England to the philosophy of educational methods and to such psychological truths as underlie all rules of teaching, and give validity to them. Such works as those of Spencer and Herbart are studied by the best of the professors, and an attempt is made to give to the student leading principles which he must work out and develop in a prescribed order. This theory is entirely right; but it seemed to me that in practice it sometimes restrained the spontaneity and inventiveness of the students, and led them to suppose that all lessons of a given character ought to be shaped to one pattern, and developed in one particular manner. For example, in one college the principle is laid down that in an observation or object lesson there should be three stages—the *presentative,* the *representative,* and the *thought* stage. The thing discussed must first be seen, and, if possible, handled, and the scholar made to tell all he can observe about it. Then in the second stage the words, technical or otherwise, which represent the various properties and incidents of the object, have to be explained; and, lastly, there should be intelligent exercise on the meaning and drift of what has been learned. Now, there

AND TRAINING COLLEGES. 83

is undoubtedly a true philosophy underlying this rule, and a little reflection on it is well calculated to rebuke the very common practice of untrained teachers, who begin every lesson with a formidable explanation of all the hard words they are going to use, instead of, first of all, evolving the facts, and afterwards giving the technical terms which connote the facts. But the student who is obliged to keep this "counsel of perfection" perpetually before her, and to cast every lesson in the same mould, loses a great many opportunities of present- ing truth in new and effective ways. It seemed to me, as I listened to some of the sketches of lessons which had been prepared, and to several of the criticism lessons in normal schools, that the students were rather too much enslaved by formulas. The young teacher who gave the lesson in the presence of the principal and her fellow-students was too much hampered by the fear of departing from the prescribed order; the students who criticised seemed only concerned to notice whether the order had been observed. A lesson on a knife began by letting the children take the article in hand and say in succession, "I have a knife, it has two parts, a handle and a blade; the blade is sharp; it will cut," etc. Then its hardness and smoothness and other qualities came into review, and then followed a little talk about the uses of a knife and the care which should be exercised in using it. But the question what was steel made of, or how it was manufactured did not arise. It was "beyond the grade." In like manner I heard several lessons on a flower, on an eagle, etc., and, although the teacher very patiently strove to make the children one by one tell all they could about it, the lessons mainly helped them to recount what they would have known without teaching, and did not carry them much forwarder. All the criticisms of the students were on the method only, "How far did the lesson illustrate in its order and development the principles which had been laid down by the college lecturer?" The question which would first occur to an English student in a criticism lesson, "What have the children learned which they did not know before?" was not asked. In several other ways I observed that minute pains had been taken to furnish an outline or pattern of the way in which a given lesson, say, a biography, a grammatical term, colonization, or the geography of a river, ought to be developed ; and that the students were then invited to take a cognate topic, and fashion a lesson on the same model. The practice is unquestionably valuable, and might with great advantage be more frequently adopted in our own training colleges at home. But unless care is exercised it has a tendency to degenerate into routine, and by leading the student to suppose that all lessons of a particular kind should only be given in one way, to discourage all independent efforts to discover still better ways. The avenues of access to the under-

AND TRAINING COLLEGES.   85

standing and sympathy of a child are many, and have not all been found out yet. It is possible to have a very logical method and yet to give a very ineffective lesson.

Some other of the plans adopted in good normal schools also deserve notice. There is the method of "*questioning practice*," which differs in many ways from an ordinary criticism lesson, and yet has the same object in view. A lecture is given by the professor, and several of the students are selected on the next day to question the whole class upon its subject, each taking one portion, so as to cover the entire ground traversed by the lecturer. Two or three other students are afterwards called on in succession to comment on the style and effectiveness of the questions, and the presiding officer sums up with observations both on the questioners and their critics.

Platform exercises also furnish a useful form of discipline. The authorities at one of the Massachusetts normal schools state in their programme:

"No efforts are spared to train the pupils to habits of self-reliance. It is to this end that special importance is attached to the platform exercises. These occupy a half-hour or so every day, and during this period pupils volunteer, each for five minutes or more, to read or recite, or to talk to the school upon any subject which they may have chosen. At such a time they have constantly to meet the criticism and questions of teachers and fellow-pupils ; and thus the exercise has been found to be valuable, not only in training the pupils to use the English language with facility and force, and to speak with distinctness and accuracy, but in bringing them to face the sort of difficulties that they may be expected to meet in their profession. On Wednesdays the apprentices have exclusive possession of the platform, and on each such occasion they give to the school the results of their past week's experience in teaching."

In view of the annual ceremonial at the end of the academic year, when the leading local authorities and the public always assemble in great numbers, the students

Public declamation of themes and essays.

are encouraged to prepare original essays on subjects selected by themselves, and the best of these are publicly recited. Among the subjects handled by the students at one such ceremony at which I was present were : "A Few Characteristics of German Schools ; School Hygiene ; Richter's Levana ; the Savagery of Childhood ; Tree-Planting at the School ; Furniture and Decoration of the Schoolroom ; the School—monarchy or republic ; Locke's Views on Education ; the Physical Basis of Brainwork ; Rosmini's Ruling Principles of Method ; Some Disadvantages of the Inductive Method of Teaching; Methods of Teaching Writing; Children's Make-believes."

Considering how very small a proportion of the

American teachers undergo this discipline, it is interesting to inquire what substitutes exist, and by what means the deficiency of normal training is supplied. *Substitutes for regular training—"The Cadet System."* In Chicago, where the school authority gave up its normal school as unnecessary, what is called the "Cadet System" has been adopted in its stead. Young people who have passed through the high school are provisionally admitted to teach for a few weeks the lower classes of a primary school, without pay. If they show promise they are temporarily engaged at 75 cents per day, for a short time, and are required to attend on Saturday classes held by one of the assistant superintendents, who takes in turn the teachers of one grade after another and instructs them in the method applicable to it. After a few weeks' attendance at such a class, and after passing the examination, the candidate receives a diploma from the school superintendent, and becomes recognized as one of the staff for the city schools. At Grand Rapids, in the State of Michigan, the "Cadet System" has also superseded the regular training school for resident graduates of the high schools. "This plan assigns young persons desiring to fit themselves for the profession as assistants to principals of schools, who supervise their practice work in the lower grades of the school. The city superintendent recommends that these cadets be instructed as a class in the principles and methods of teaching and then be assigned to work them out

88 NOTES ON AMERICAN SCHOOLS

for themselves; and if the work of a year fails to develop fairly good teachers, they are dropped altogether from the rolls."

Normal classes. Normal classes are often conducted by the school superintendent or under his authority, with a view to professional improvement, and to the discussion and illustration of school methods and discipline. Lectures of a higher and more speculative kind are given by some of the abler school superintendents, and attendance on these is voluntary. The following is a syllabus of a course of lectures on the history of education, and on modern educational theories, given by Mr. MacAlister, the city superintendent in Philadelphia. It illustrates well the desire of some of the leading educational authorities of America to give a scientific character to the study of education; and to find, by means of the investigation of the history and philosophy of the subject, a sound and safe basis for practical rules.

"1. THE RISE OF MODERN EDUCATION. The decay of classical culture. Condition of society and education in the Middle Ages. Foundation of universities. Revival of learning. Invention of printing. Bacon and the inductive philosophy. Humanism and the scientific spirit. Change in man's relation to nature. Revolution in method of thinking. Influence of these changes upon education and schools. Humanistic education. Beginning of schools for the people.

AND TRAINING COLLEGES.

"2. COMENIUS, THE FOUNDER OF THE NEW EDUCATION. Sketch of his life. His application of the Baconian philosophy to educational problems. Educational writings. Pansophic scheme. Educational theories : 1. Methodology ; 2. System of school organization ; 3. Foundation of primary education. Influence of Comenius on the progress of education.

"3. THE ENGLISH REFORMERS. The Humanistic movement in England. The views of Erasmus. The Humanistic leaders—John Colet, Sir Thomas More, Roger Ascham, Richard Mulcaster. Influence of Bacon on the realistic spirit. John Milton's theory of education. John Locke : his philosophy of mind and its relation to educational method ; his educational theories. Locke's place as an educational reformer.

"4. ROUSSEAU, THE PREACHER OF NATURALISM IN EDUCATION. Condition of society and state of education in his time. His view of human nature. Activity of educational thought. *Émile :* discussion of its educational doctrines ; fundamental principles ; subjects to be taught ; methods of instruction. Rousseau's influence upon educational theory and practice.

"5. PESTALOZZI, THE APOSTLE OF EDUCATIONAL REFORM. His life and experiments as a teacher. The essential principles of his method : symmetrical development of all the powers of body and mind ; training of sense perception ; self-activity of the mind ; observation ; the order and development of training ; acquisition and expression ; discipline. Pestalozzi's place in modern pedagogy. His influence upon theoretical and practical education.

" 6. FRÖBEL, THE PHILOSOPHER OF CHILDHOOD. Fundamental principles of his philosophy of education. His extension of Pestalozzi's method. His philosophy of child nature. The kindergarten. The gifts and occupations—their meaning and use. Influence of Fröbel's philosophy upon general education. Its relations to family life ; to elementary methods of instruction ; to manual training ; to discipline ; to social progress."

A belief in the paramount importance of special preparation of the teacher's office, is very strong throughout all parts of America, and is daily becoming stronger and more general. This belief finds expression in many ways, notably in the existence of institutes, teachers' associations and conventions, and in reading circles.

Teachers' Institutes.

By an "Institute" is meant a sort of normal class, held periodically for the teachers of a district, and furnishing instruction in the art and practice of education, and an opportunity for the discussion of methods. Institutes are, in fact, migratory and occasional academies, and they were brought into existence before any regular normal schools were founded. The first meeting of this

AND TRAINING COLLEGES.

kind was held in Hartford, in Connecticut, as far back as 1839, by Henry Barnard, who was the Secretary to the State Board of Education, and who gathered together twenty-six young teachers in the public schools, and provided for them, during several weeks, a course of lectures, reviewing the topics usually taught in the common schools, together with instruction in method, supplemented by visits of observation to the public schools of the city. I ought, in passing, to say how much the literature of education owes to Mr. Barnard, who has during a long life spent himself, and, I fear, much of his fortune too, in efforts to reprint costly works and monographs on education. It was a great pleasure to me to see this educational veteran at a meeting of teachers in Rhode Island last autumn, and to find him still, in his honored old age, as keenly interested as ever in the advancement of educational science, and in the practical improvement of scholastic methods. The example he set was imitated at first in a rather fitful and hesitating way, but afterwards more systematically. The earliest of these gatherings were purely voluntary on the part of the teachers, and grew out of the endeavor to qualify themselves for their work; but soon, during the first decade, several of the New England States began to make it an obligation on the young teachers to attend them, and to place the management of them in the charge of the school superintendents, or other officers appointed for the purpose. By degrees the system spread, at first to the Southern, and afterwards to the Western States, and the "Teachers' Institute" is now a recognized factor in the educational system throughout the Union, and in the Dominion of Canada. The *data* for any safe general statement in reference to them are somewhat scattered, diverse, and obscure. In a few States institutes are not legally required to be held at all ; in some, institutes are incorporated into State or district systems, and in others into county systems. In some they are held under State authority, and in others under local authority. In some cases the expenses are paid by State funds, in others by county funds, in others by contributions from the teachers, and in others by the fees for teachers' licenses. In some cases the institutes are held at a fixed time, when the schools are closed, and in others they are held at any time the local authorities may choose, and when the schools are in session ; in some, the schools are closed during the sessions of the institute, in others they remain open. In some the teachers are paid for attending, or fined for not attending ; in others neither course is pursued. Some of them are held by voluntary or private persons, and others—now by far the greater number—by the official superintendent of the district, or under his direction. The time devoted to them also varies materially. In many States provision is made for an annual session of

AND TRAINING COLLEGES. 93

from three to six days, and in a few for a session of two, or even three weeks. In other States the teachers are required to meet monthly, or once in two months, for two or three hours in the evening or on Saturday.

But, though diverse in all these respects, the object to be attained, and the method of attaining it are practically uniform. They are designed, in the first place, and mainly, for the help of the large number of teachers who have not been trained in normal seminaries; and, in the second place, for helping those who have been so trained. "Their aim," says the last report of the Commissioner, "is to revive the spirit and confidence of teachers, awaken a pride in the profession, stimulate to self-improvement, and by a progressive course of study and instruction review the branches taught in the schools, and increase the practical requirements of the teachers." Accordingly it is the duty of each official school superintendent, or district inspector, to classify the teachers of his district, and to gather into their several classes those who take up the work of each grade. A young teacher, it must be observed, is, on admission, examined and certified, with a view to her service in a class of a given grade. She cannot take charge of a higher class without a further examination, and a higher diploma. While attached to a particular class, it is her duty to attend the lessons at the institute specially adapted to the work of that particular grade, so that in each department the young people are receiving instruction in method, in so far as it is applicable to the work of their own classes. Besides this, collective instruction is given occasionally on larger questions relating to the general principles of teaching and organization. But, on the whole, it may be said that "institutes," in the American sense, while not designed in any way to supersede regular normal training, furnish, in many cases, a useful supplement to it, and in many more help, in an appreciable degree, to supply the lack of such training.

Besides these local institutes, which are essentially normal classes, engaged in a good deal of merely technical work, there are in America other and larger organizations, of a wholly voluntary kind, which, though mainly, are not exclusively composed of teachers, and which seek to elucidate the higher and more general aspects of education ; and to bring the teaching profession into due relations with all the more advanced thought of the country, with the professors of her universities, and with the best of her writers and her clergy. Foremost among these was the New England Association of Teachers, which has subsequently changed its name to the American Institute of Instruction. It was founded in 1830 at Boston, and the first meeting attended by 300 persons, chiefly from the Eastern States, was presided over

AND TRAINING COLLEGES.

by the well-known Dr. Wayland, the President of Brown University. In his introductory address he struck the keynote of the whole enterprise, and foreshadowed, with keen insight, the future history of an Association, which, after fifty-eight years of growth, is to-day more flourishing and influential than ever. He said :

"In the long train of her joyous anniversaries, New England has yet beheld no one more illustrious than this. We have assembled to-day, not to proclaim how well our fathers have done, but to inquire how we may enable her sons to do better. . . . We have come up here, to the City of the Pilgrims, to ask how we may render their children more worthy of their ancestors, and more pleasing to their God. We meet to give to each other the right hand of fellowship in carrying forward this all-important work, and here to leave our professional pledge, that if the succeeding generations do not act worthily the guilt shall not rest upon those who are now the instructors of New England."

In the four days during which the meeting lasted, these were the subjects discussed :—Physical education ; the development of the intellectual faculties in connection with the teaching of geography ; the infant school system ; the spelling of words, and a rational method of teaching their meaning ; lyceums and literary societies, and their connection with the school ; practical methods of teaching rhetoric, geometry and algebra ; the monitorial system ;

vocal music; classical learning; arithmetic; the construction and furnishing of schoolrooms. Very early in the history of the Association it was resolved that the clergy of all denominations, and the representatives of the press in the neighborhood in which the meeting was held, should be invited. Among the lecturers who spoke before the Association, during its early years, I find the names of Jacob Abbott, whose books many of us delighted in as children; of Noah Webster, the lexicographer; of George Ticknor; of Spurzheim, the German philosopher; of Calhoun, the statesman, who lectured on the duties of school committees; of Lowell Mason, who advocated the introduction of music into the common school; of Judge Story, on the Science of Government as a branch of general education; of Ralph Waldo Emerson, on the best mode of inspiring a correct taste in English literature; of Horace Mann, on the necessity of previous study to parents and teachers; of John Philbrick, on school government; of George Sumner, on the state of education in some countries of Europe; of Gideon Thayer, on the means of awakening in the minds of parents a deeper interest in the education of their children; of Miss Peabody, on Kindergarten, the Gospel for children; and of Henry Ward Beecher, on the New Profession. From the numerous other topics treated at these annual meetings, I select a few characteristic examples :

AND TRAINING COLLEGES.

The study of the classics; training the human voice; the number of hours a day to be devoted to instruction; the sources of personal power; the self-education of the teacher; the legitimate influence of schools on commerce, on agriculture, on manufactures, on civil polity, and on morals; the cultivation of a sense of honor among pupils; the right and wrong use of text-books; the rights of the taught; oral teaching; the co-education of the sexes; drawing not an accomplishment, but a language for the graphic representation of facts, and as a means of developing taste; psychology in relation to teaching.

As I look down through the annals of this Association, I am struck with two or three facts: (1) That it has succeeded in enlisting the coöperation and sympathy, not only of teachers of all ranks, from the primary school to the university, but of many of the most prominent thinkers, public writers, clergy, statesmen, and lawyers in the States. (2) That its peripatetic character has enabled it from year to year to break new ground, to awaken new local interest, and to exercise a sort of missionary influence on the improvement of education throughout the whole country. (3) That the subjects of discussion are mainly practical, and have a direct bearing on the improvements of school methods; but that many of them are of a larger and more speculative kind, selected with a view to broaden the intellectual horizon of the members,

and to find new meeting-points between the world
of the schoolroom and the world of thought and
of industrial and intellectual activity outside of the
school.   (4) That in all the topics of discussion I
fail to find one which touches the question of the
payment of the teacher or his pecuniary or professional interests.

I had the great pleasure last year of attending
the fifty-eighth annual gathering of this
thriving Association.   At Newport, in
Rhode Island, there were assembled during four
days about a thousand members, including the
teachers of primary and grammar schools, the professors in the chief colleges and universities in the
New England States, the principal teachers and
authorities of the normal schools, and nearly all
the school superintendents and official inspectors ;
besides a few public men, such as the Mayor of
Newport, and the State Commissioner, members
of School Boards and Committees, and the like.
There were animated meetings at the beginning
and end of each day, for lectures and addresses on
the more general popular aspects of education, and
throughout the day sectional meetings, in three or
four groups, for papers and discussions on special
topics.   A simple and touching religious exercise
introduced each day's proceedings, and there was
at times hearty choral singing, which, with one or
two excursions at the end, constituted the only dis-
sipations of the assemblage.   The subjects were of

AND TRAINING COLLEGES. 99

the same general character as I have already described, and I was especially struck in observing
the terms of perfect freedom and equality subsist-
ing between the teachers of all classes, and the
public officials concerned in the administration of
the various State systems.

Another very characteristic meeting at which I
had the opportunity of being present, The College
was that of the College Associations of Association of the Middle
Pennsylvania, now enlarged in its scope States.
so as to include the Colleges and Universities of
the Middle States and Maryland. It was held in
the magnificent University buildings in Philadelphia, and after an address of welcome from the
Provost of the University, proceeded to discuss
seriously, during two or three days, a number of
topics especially concerned with higher education :
For example, the Place of History in a College
Course; the Influence of Endowments on Education;
the German University of To-day ; Post-graduate
Courses ; Pedagogics as a Part of a College Curriculum, and the Education of Women in Colleges ;
the Proper Requirements for Admission to a College
Course. The treatment of the setopics was serious,
and both scientific and practical ; there was full
recognition of great principles, and yet an anxious
attempt to see those principles in the light of the
actual problems of a professor's life.

An equally significant experience awaited us
when we crossed the northern boundary of the

100   NOTES ON AMERICAN SCHOOLS

State of Maine, and found ourselves in the Dominion of Canada. At St. John, New Brunswick, was held last July a convention of all the teachers of the maritime provinces of New Brunswick, Nova Scotia, and Prince Edward's Island. Here, again, the gathering comprehended teachers of all ranks, from the primary teacher to the university principal and professor, the State superintendents, all the inspectors of schools, and a number of public men. Sir William Dawson came from Montreal, and the Governor of New Brunswick, the Premiers of the three provinces, and one of the Ministers of the Dominion also took part in the proceedings. There were some twelve hundred persons at the opening and closing meetings. But the sectional discussions throughout the day were largely attended, and were concerned with many important points of detail, which were earnestly debated. There was a special section devoted to the investigation of infant teaching and discipline, and at this meeting some papers, read by female teachers of experience, were of unusual merit and suggestiveness. Another section devoted itself to the consideration of the work of normal schools ; another to questions relating to the teaching of different branches of natural science ; another to the right ornamentation, furnishing, and equipment of the common school, and to the right use of its playgrounds and accessories ; and another to the con-

The Convention of the Maritime Provinces of Canada.

sideration of modes of inspecting and examining school organization and work. It was impossible not to observe here, in Canada, as well as in the States, how much of stimulus and encouragement teachers, especially the younger members of the profession, derived from these gatherings ; how many new and germinating ideas were disseminated, how many valuable friendships were formed, and to how large an extent public opinion, both within and without the profession, was helped, strengthened, and ennobled. The free interchange of thought and experience between the teachers and the officials who are charged with the supervision and administration of schools, struck me as especially valuable, and has evidently done much to promote that cordial coöperation of teachers and inspectors in the discharge of a great public duty, which is so noticeable both in the Union and in Canada. All through the Dominion of Canada, as well as through the States of the Union, scores of such local meetings are to be found seriously at work during the first, second, and third weeks of the summer holiday ; and I was very deeply impressed to see such eager and enthusiastic companies of hard-worked teachers, who, after a long session, and in the hot weather of July, voluntarily dedicated the first few days of their well-earned vacation to self-improvement and to professional fellowship. It must be owned that the American has a genius for organizing conventions, and that

102   NOTES ON AMERICAN SCHOOLS

all sections of the community find greater delight in attending them than we of the old world are wont to experience.⏋The popularity of such conventions seems to increase year by year. There is now, besides the various local gatherings in States, and in groups of States, a National Educational Association, which organizes every year a collective meeting on a huge scale, at some great centre, one year at Chicago, another at Boston, another at St. Louis, and last year at San Francisco. Some thousands of teachers spent three, four, or five days in travelling across the continent from different parts, in order to attend the grand congress, which lasted from the 17th to the 28th of July. The programme is very elaborate including provision for receptions, sections, departments, subcommittees, concerts, public harangues and excursions. Such great gatherings are suited to the soil, and fit in better with the habits and social arrangements of America than with those of England. But I think they grow out of a genuine zeal for the improvement of education, and out of a republican sentiment that every man who has got anything good to say, or has made a useful invention or discovery, is bound to communicate it to his fellow-teachers, and to invite their criticisms upon it.

I have elsewhere * described the curious, but very characteristic American institution known

---

* In the *Nineteenth Century* for October, 1888.

AND TRAINING COLLEGES.

as the Chautauqua Summer Assembly. In the remote north-west corner of the great State of New York, a clearance has been made in the "forest primæval," and near the shore of a little lake. Here, during July and August, may be seen an encampment of from eight to ten thousand persons, living in ténts or wooden cottages, and forming themselves daily into classes, reading parties, working in laboratories, studying in small companies in a library, or listening to lectures. They have a number of separate rooms for different kinds of study or manual work, a gymnasium, and a vast amphitheatre rudely fashioned on the curved slope of a hill, with a roof, and one wall on the side on which there is an organ and a platform, but otherwise open to the air and the woods. It is one of the most memorable and affecting of my American experiences to have addressed 6,000 people in this sheltered place, to have heard their voices as they uplifted a psalm, while the ancient trees waved and rustled all round them in the summer twilight, and to have witnessed the hearty enthusiasm wherewith the whole of this large company, comprising persons of all ages, shared the simple recreations of the place, and yet seemed all bent on efforts after self-improvement. This assembly is the parent of many similar local assemblies, and the headquarters of a vast organization, extending through the whole length and breadth of the Union, and of the Canadian Domin-

NOTES ON AMERICAN SCHOOLS

ion, and known as the Chautauqua Reading Circle. Its members, upwards of 100,000 in number, are scattered all over the American Continent, and their one tie of association is that they all pledge themselves to read every year a certain set of four or five books, to write papers in form of *résumé*, criticism, or account of what they have read, and when opportunity offers, to meet from time to time, to read the books together, to discuss their contents, and, if possible, to obtain from some competent professor or schoolmaster an occasional lecture in the elucidation of the prescribed book. It has been a remarkably successful enterprise, has developed among many persons who have had few opportunities of early study, a sense of intellectual fellowship with other self-taught and striving students, and has exercised a far-reaching influence on the mental life and thought of the American people. The whole movement began eighteen years ago in the form of a voluntary association of teachers chiefly connected with Sunday-schools, who met together for the study of the Bible, and for mutual conference about the best mode of giving religious instruction. Very soon it was found that masters and mistresses employed in the primary schools and grammar schools of the States wished to associate themselves with the Assembly ; and the *Teachers' Retreat* was organized, partly for summer rest and congenial fellowship, but mainly for the systematic reading of the best educational

AND TRAINING COLLEGES.

literature, and for the discussion of the methods and processes of education. So, during the two months of the Assembly, about two weeks are annually appropriated to the members of the teaching profession, and year by year the number of such persons to be found at Chautauqua increases. Out of this experiment grew in time a *Teachers' Reading Union,* for the benefit of those who were too widely scattered to give personal attendance at the meeting. This department of the whole work of the institution is separately organized.

It suggests the names of suitable books, facilitates the circulation of them among the members, provides three regular and several advanced courses of professional reading ; the book-work being supplemented by written correspondence, and records of experience, and by special counsels forwarded by the professors to the members. For the annual fee of one dollar, each member is entitled to receive during the year seven such communications in answer to questions, or in explanation of difficulties.

This example has been extensively followed. The "Teachers' Reading Circle" is now recognized everywhere as the most valuable agency for the improvement of the rural schools, and as a humble, but not ineffective, substitute for normal training. The report of the Commissioner of Education says that, in the case of country teachers, "Whatever knowledge

106   NOTES ON AMERICAN SCHOOLS

they obtain of the theory of teaching, and whatever promptings they receive to enter on the study of mind, and to learn something of the laws of its growth, may be set down largely to the credit of the reading circle." President Allyn, of Illinois, says, "The work of the teachers' reading circles is in the direction of healthful mental and moral progress. No one can read a good book without profit, and when such a book is in the line of one's life-work, it is both inspiration and motive power." As these views have prevailed, the system has, during the last seven or eight years, been largely extended. Ohio and Wisconsin were among the earliest States to form State Teachers' Reading Circles, Indiana soon followed, and at present more than twenty States have formally adopted the plan. It is estimated that at least 75,000 teachers in the United States are reading, methodically and systematically, works bearing upon professional and general culture.

I abridge from the last report presented to Congress by the Commissioner of Education the following particulars respecting the formation and work of these associations :—

"The objects of the State Teachers' Reading Circles are substantially the same, namely, the improvement of the members in literary, scientific, and professional knowledge, and the promotion of habits of self-culture. This end is sought by prescribing a certain course of study, securing books

AND TRAINING COLLEGES.

at reduced rates, preparing lists of the best educational publications, by offering advice and direction as to the methods of reading and study, by examinations of the work done, and by certificates of proficiency.

" The act of organizing the State Circle has generally been accomplished at the annual assembly of the State Teachers' Associations, and the work is usually carried on under the control of this association. Directors, boards of management, etc., are chosen, who map out the course and direct the work of the circle. County and local circles are also formed, subsidiary to the general or State circle, and even individual members may pursue the course alone.

" The conditions of membership are liberal, any teacher or other person being received who promises to pursue the prescribed course of study, and pays the small fee—usually 25 cents, or 50 cents annually. Meetings of local circles for conference, discussion, and review are held once a week in some States, and bi-weekly in others. The course of study is usually outlined and published in the educational journals, and in the county papers.

"In the preparation of these outlines, a department of study is under the special supervision of some member of the State Board. The object of this study is twofold, namely, professional and general culture. As for the prominence given to one or the other of these subjects, that is determined by the actual needs of the teachers. The fourth year's reading (1886–87) for the Ohio Teachers' Reading Circle is given herewith, to indicate the general scope of such studies.

"I. *Psychology.*—'Sully's Teachers' Handbook of Psychology.'

"II. *Literature.*—'Hamlet,' and 'As You Like It.' Selections from Wordsworth.

"III. *History.*—Barnes' 'Brief General History of the World,' or Thalheimer's 'General History.'

"IV. *Political Economy.*—Gregory's 'Political Economy,' or Chapin's 'First Principles of Political Economy,' with at least one educational periodical.

"In a majority of the States provision is made for stated examinations of the work performed, and certificates are awarded with diplomas upon completion of the course.

"The *Union Reading Circle*, a paper published in the interest of this work, reports (June, 1887) three new societies in Georgia, two in Kentucky, five in Iowa, and twelve others in as many different States. Memorial days are now the fashion; the poets Bryant, Longfellow, and Tennyson, with Dickens and other literary men, receiving their share of honor in various places. The Agassiz Society of Philadelphia promises to make the summer vacation an opportunity for scientific research and study, and each one will contribute towards the common museum. The Gesenius, a

AND TRAINING COLLEGES. 109

new circle of Cleveland, makes Hebrew a specialty, as the Xenophon Society carries on the systematic study of Greek. The Curtis Society of Buffalo, N. Y., studies politics, and discusses all questions of reform. The Tulane Home Study and Reading Society is organized, with headquarters at Tulane University, New Orleans, La.

" Besides the State associations, others claiming a national character have been organized. In 1885 the Teachers' National Reading Circle was legally incorporated under the laws of New York. Prof. W. H. Payne, of Michigan, was chosen President, supported by 18 directors, constituting the official board. This organization provides 18 courses of reading, 6 being professional, 3 in general culture, and 9 non-professional. In the first, 27 books are recommended. Each course includes 3 groups of studies, 2 books in each group, and any course (3 books for the year) may be taken by the reader. Diplomas will be granted to the members who pass the three different examinations in some one prescribed course, and who prepare an accepted thesis on some educational topic connected with the reading. . . . One or two of the educational departments of Canada prescribe a course of reading for teachers, purely voluntary, and hence followed by no examinations. The department provides, however, that 'should the teachers of any inspectorial division agree to read the course with this end in view, and should the county board of examiners make adequate provision for such examination, the department would recognize, by special certificate, this additional element of professional culture.'"

It will be observed that all the organizations I have described — local institutes, general conventions, reading circles, teachers' retreats—set before them two objects, and two objects only, self-improvement, and the improvement of education. There is a remarkable absence in America of discussions on what may be called the politics of education, or on the means of obtaining professional influence outside the profession itself. And it is to this singleness of purpose, to the essentially practical aim of the great gatherings of teachers, that one may fairly attribute the interest which is universally shown in them, the warm and respectful welcome which they receive from parents and local authorities as they itinerate from town to town, the large share of importance assigned to the meetings in the local press, and the extent to which the influence of the teaching body has steadily been enlarged during the last 60 years. Public opinion, after all, evinces a true instinct when it shows—as it always does—a certain distrust of trading and professional associations, obviously designed to keep up the scale of remuneration, to assert corporate rights and privileges, or otherwise to protect class interests. It has a suspicion that these interests

AND TRAINING COLLEGES. 111

are not necessarily or always identical with the
larger interests of the community. But it recognizes and rightly recognizes the national importance of any efforts by which teachers as a body
seek to understand and to do their work better;
and to keep themselves in due *rapport* with the
communities whose needs they seek to supply.

All through the States there is a much greater
demand for educational literature than in England;
and even the more philosophical treatises on education, such as those of Herbert Spencer, Alexander Bain, and Professor Sully, are eagerly and
largely read. I cannot help thinking that the
strong professional feeling which seems to incor-
porate all classes of teachers, and to make them
and the public officials conscious of a common
interest in educational progress, is one of the most
encouraging and hopeful signs of the times.

It would be beyond the special purpose of these
notes, which concern themselves mainly
with such observations as may possibly   Colleges.
prove suggestive to the teachers in our own training
colleges and elementary schools, to do more than
barely mention any facts relating to higher schools
and colleges. But many institutions recently built
and endowed by private munificence possess a splen-
dor and completeness of equipment rarely seen on
this side of the Atlantic. New universities and
colleges are being created yearly. The three great
colleges for women—Wellesley, Vassar, and Bryn

Mawr—are amply supplied with laboratories, art galleries, and every modern appliance for effective teaching, and are surrounded by extensive and beautiful grounds. There were enumerated in the last official returns of the 38 States of the Union no less than 491 distinct institutions for higher education, of which 283 were universities, colleges, and higher schools, 75 were colleges for women, and 133 were professional schools, chiefly theological or medical, but unconnected with universities. Every one of these 491 institutions possesses the right to confer degrees. This right is in each case granted in a charter by the Governor and legislature of the State in which the college is situated, and is very easily obtained by almost any superior school of fair repute. The degrees are conferred by the professors and teachers without external examination or criticism. There is no common standard of qualification; nearly every student who passes with fair credit through the three or four required years "graduates" as a matter of course. The conception of a "University" as an organization apart from a college and entitled to apply a uniform and impartial test to students who have been taught under different conditions, does not exist in America. The difference in the conditions which govern universities and academic organization in general in England and in America will be best understood by considering that in all there are only five public bodies in England and Wales,

AND TRAINING COLLEGES.   113

four in Scotland, and three in Ireland, which are
empowered by charter from the Crown to confer
academical degrees.   In Oxford or Cambridge
the university exists, in a certain sense, indepen-
dently of the several colleges associated with it,
subjects all the students to the same examination,
and confers degrees that have a recognized meaning
and value.   The University of London receives
from all parts of the Kingdom students of all
classes, whether taught in colleges or not, and
after a series of examinations, gives the titles of
Bachelor, Master or Doctor, in the several faculties
of art, science, medicine, laws and literature.   The
degree has in every case a fixed and well-known
connotation.   No purely professional corporation,
e. g., a medical school, is empowered to give the
title of Doctor.   Hence, M.D. in England is a
title conferred by a university alone, and always
signifies that besides professional qualification, the
holder has received a liberal education.   The universities of the United Kingdom have of late
added to their special academic work the important function of testing and certifying the results of
instruction in the secondary and high schools in all
parts of the country.   By means of local examinations, a standard of requirement has been set up
for junior and senior candidates of 15 to 18
years of age, and thousands of pupils in the higher
schools who are not destined for the universities
are annually certified to have reached this standard.

8

But there is nothing analogous to this in the United States, and there are therefore no data for a comparison of the value of degrees in that country and in our own. Here, at least, the public know well what a university degree or certificate means, because it is granted by an independent and detached body. In America each separate institution which has the power to grant distinctions may have its own scheme of study, and lay down its own conditions of graduation, and the public have no means of knowing whether those conditions are leniently or stringently enforced. As with the public schools, so also with colleges and universities, the educational authority is in every case entirely isolated and local, and no means exist for comparing the achievements of one such body with those of another, or with any common standard of efficiency. Parents and the public are therefore compelled to accept the account of its work which each institution gives of itself. They are unable to check that account by reference to any external and responsible authority or by any recognized test of acquirement. The consequence is that degrees, as such, unless obtained at one of the seven or eight universities of the highest rank, as Harvard, Yale, or at Baltimore, are of no value in the States and mean very little. It is manifest that the American system helps to promote the general diffusion of knowledge among those who have passed the school age; but it is equally manifest

AND TRAINING COLLEGES. 115

that it helps to dignify with academic titles the
kind of work which in Europe would be done in
gymnasia, in *lycées,* or in grammar schools, and that
it somewhat discourages the attainment of a high
standard of scholarship.

The one great safeguard, however, for the continued and rapid improvement of education in America is the universal
interest shown in it by the community. There is
no matter of public concern more keenly and
frequently debated. Any complaint of negligence
or inefficiency in connection with the schools
rouses the indignation of parents and excites general discussion. There is everywhere manifest an
eager, almost a restless, desire to effect improvements and to try new experiments. The immense
commercial prosperity of America, no doubt, causes
many persons there, as elsewhere, to take a merely
material view of the purposes and uses of education. But there is no lack of loftier and more
generous ideals. For example, I know no wiser or
more felicitous description of the true aim of a
school than is contained in the words of President
Adams of Cornell University, when he says, " The
main object of education is not merely the acquisition of information; it is not even the development of the faculties; it is, or ought to be, the
awakening of certain desires that will serve to the
pupil as a sort of perpetual inspiration through
life." This is, I believe, an ideal vividly present

116   NOTES ON AMERICAN SCHOOLS

to the minds of many of the leading men and
women of America, and one which is every day
likely to be more nearly realized.

To any observer who is interested in the social
and intellectual progress of the race, and who
cares to understand the forces which are shaping
the character and fortunes of the coming generations, a visit to America is an exhilarating experience. The atmosphere, both moral and physical,
is eminently stimulating. The signs of energy
and enterprise, of hopefulness and boundless promise, meet the eye in every direction. "Every
American," said to me one of the leading clergymen in Boston, "every American is an optimist."
He cannot help being so. He has at his command
vast and undeveloped material resources. He is
conscious, in himself and in his countrymen, of
ambition and enthusiasm, of the ability to sur-
mount difficulties, and of yet unused intellectual
strength. His golden age lies in the future, not in
the past. He does not indulge in the English-
man's habit of self-depreciation. He never falls
into the mood in which his English cousin is often
fain to disparage the institutions of his own country, and to assume that educational or other work
is better done by foreigners than by himself. He
believes that Englishmen are only half sincere
when they use such language. But if he is sometimes boastful, it is because he feels secure in the
conviction that he can justify his boasts. He is

AND TRAINING COLLEGES.

aware of many of the defects in his own educational system, especially its frequent lack of thoroughness, and he is very sensible of the need for amendment. But he is not disheartened, for in the first place he believes that he is fully able to effect improvement, and in the second place he means to do it.

118   NOTES ON AMERICAN SCHOOLS

SCHEMES OF GRADED INSTRUCTION IN PRIMARY

AGE.	ENGLAND.	NEW YORK.	PHILADELPHIA.
Under 7.	(*a.*) *Elements* of reading, writing, and arithmetic. (*b.*) *Lessons* on objects, the phenomena of nature and of common life. (*c.*) *Appropriate* and varied m a n u a l employments. *Singing.* *Needlework* (girls).	*Language.*—R e a d ing; spelling; exercises in combining sounds, form, color, parts and uses of familiar objects. *Counting* by ones to 100, by twos to 50, backwards from 10 to 1. *Slate writing* short words. *Drawing* straight lines, vertical, oblique, etc. *Vocal music.*	*Language.* — Reading simple names of things at sight. Phonic method. Written, not oral, spelling. *Writing.* — E a s y letters and words containing them. *Conversations* about familiar things. *Arithmetic.* — A l l the four rules with numbers up to 5, with objects and figures. *Lessons* on f o r m and objects.
Under 8. Standard I.	*To read* a short paragraph from a book not confined to words of one syllable. *Copy* in manuscript characters a line of print, and write from dictation not more than 10 easy words, commencing with capital letters. *Copybooks* (large or half text hand) to be shown.	*Language.* — Reading, meaning of words, spelling, punctuation, lessons on form, color, objects. *Arithmetic.* — Adding single columns of 10 figures. Multiplying by 2. *Writing.* — Short sentences f r o m copy.	*Language.* — Reading, phonic drill, vocal drill, tone, inflection, etc. Learning simple verses. *Spelling* of common and easy words. *Writing* copy from blackboard. *Short sentences* from dictation. *Arithmetic.* — All

AND TRAINING COLLEGE. 119

SCHOOLS FOR CHILDREN FROM 6 TO 14.

AGE.	CHICAGO.	MASSACHUSETTS.	ONTARIO (FOUR STAGES).
Under 7.	*Conversation* and oral exercises. *Reading* by the "word and sentence" method. *Writing* and spelling. *Arithmetic.* — All operations with numbers up to 10. U.S. money. The inch, pint, etc. *Moulding* in clay and elementary drawing. *The musical scale.*	*Conversation* about familiar things. Use of singular and plural words. *Recitation* of "gems of poetry." *Writing* words and short sentences. *Reading* by words, not letters. *Arithmetic.*—All combinations from 1 to 10, with counters or other objects, before figures. *Geography.*—Oral lessons on wind, rain, snow, hills, valleys, springs, etc. Points of compass. *Lessons* on color and form, and linear drawing.	
Under 8. Standard I.	*Reading.*—Oral exercises in the use of verbs. *Copying* and writing capitals. *Combination* of numbers up to 60. Notation up to 1,000. Elementary fractions. Tables. *Music* by note. *Drawing* in two dimensions.	*Oral lessons* on plants, animals, color, etc. *Writing.* — Copy short sentences from blackboard. *Reading.* — Phonic drill on elementary sounds. *Form* and meaning of words in sentences (only one new word in a sentence).	First reading book. *Spelling* from reading lessons on slates, and orally. *Numeration* to 1,000. Addition and subtraction. *Linear drawing.* *Geography.* — Conversational lessons about the earth.

120 NOTES ON AMERICAN SCHOOLS

SCHEMES OF GRADED INSTRUCTION IN PRIMARY

AGE.	ENGLAND.	NEW YORK.	PHILADELPHIA.
Under 8. Standard I.	*Notation* and numeration up to 1,000. Simple addition and subtraction of numbers of not more than three figures. In addition not more than five lines to be given. The multiplication table to 6 times 12. *To repeat* 20 lines of simple verse. *To explain* a plan of the school and playground. The four cardinal points. The meaning and use of a map. *Needlework* and knitting (girls).	*Drawing.* — Triangles, concentric squares, etc. *Common objects* and substances.	four processes with numbers up to 20, coins, pints, yards, feet. *Drawing.*—Straight lines in various combinations. Simple designs to be invented by pupils. *Lessons* on animals and plants, and aspects of nature. Color, etc.
Under 9. Standard II.	*To read* a short paragraph from an elementary reading book. *A passage* of not more than six lines, from the same book, slowly read once, and then dictated word by word. *Copybooks* (large and half text hand) to be shown. *Notation* and numeration up to 100,000. The four simple rules to	*Language.* — Reading in books. Spelling familiar words. Exercises in place and direction. *Arithmetic.* — Written and mental up to multiplication with two figures. Federal money. *Penmanship* on paper. *Drawing.* — Hexagon, octagon, and other rectilinear figures.	*Reading.* — Recitation of short passages in prose and verse. Punctuation. *Spelling.* — Dictation. Marking of long and short vowels and silent letters. Occasional oral spelling only. *Writing* on ruled paper. Oral and written composition; short stories; letters. Words alike in sound but different in meaning.

AND TRAINING COLLEGES. 121

SCHOOLS FOR CHILDREN FROM 6 TO 14—*Cont.*

AGE.	CHICAGO.	MASSACHUSETTS.	ONTARIO (FOUR STAGES).
Under 8. Standard II.	*Oral lessons* on animals. Time by the clock. Color, etc.	*Spelling*, oral and written, of easy words. *Arithmetic.*— Numbers up to 20, and problems involving them. *Home Geography.*— Roads, rivers, etc., with map of school premises and district. *Historical* anecdotes. *Drawing* lines and angles.	*Rote singing.* *Oral exercises* in language. *Common objects,* their parts and qualities.
Under 9. Standard II.	*Oral exercises* in use of adjectives and relative pronouns (no rules or definitions); writing; spelling; reproduction of short stories. *Arithmetic,* oral and written. Elementary fractions. Weights and measures. *Geography.* — Plan of schoolroom. Cardinal points. The globe. *Music* by note.	*Oral Lessons.*—Use of personal pronouns. *Reading* from books and at sight from other books not in use in the class. Scholars to read *to the Class.* *Spelling* drill on words most commonly misspelled. *Writing* on paper. Capitals to be used. *Arithmetic.*—Calculations up to 144.	

NOTES ON AMERICAN SCHOOLS

SCHEMES OF GRADED INSTRUCTION IN PRIMARY

AGE.	ENGLAND.	NEW YORK.	PHILADELPHIA.
Under 9. Standard II	short division. The multiplication table and the pence table to 12s. *To repeat* 40 lines of poetry, and to know their meaning. *To point out* nouns and verbs. *Sewing* and knitting (girls). *The size* and shape of the world. Geographical terms simply explained and illustrated by reference to the map of England. Physical geography of hills and rivers. *Or* Elementary science.	*Sewing* in girls' classes.	*Arithmetic.* — All processes up to 144, Roman numerals. Notation up to thousands. *Geography.* — Diagram of school premises; points of compass; globe. *Drawing.* — Freehand. Rectilinear and curved figures. Object lessons.
Under 10. Standard III.	*To read* a passage from a more advanced reading book, or from stories from English history. *Six lines* from one of the reading books of the standard, slowly read once and then dictated. *Copybooks* (capitals and figures, large and small hand) to be shown. *The former rules,*	*Language.* — Reading (3d book). Oral lessons on qualities, etc., of familiar objects. Composition, spelling, meaning and use of words. *Arithmetic.* — Written and mental. Weights and measures. *Geography* (without text-books) from globes and outline maps.	*Reading.* — Phonic analysis. Recitation and composition. *Writing.* — Copybooks and copying of choice extracts in prose and verse. *Nouns and Verbs* and their use in sentences. *Arithmetic.* — All four rules to hundreds of thousands. Weights, measures, and

AND TRAINING COLLEGES.

SCHOOLS FOR CHILDREN FROM 6 TO 14—*Cont.*

AGE.	CHICAGO.	MASSACHUSETTS.	ONTARIO (FOUR STAGES).
Under 9. Standard III.	*Drawing.* — Leaves and simple solids. *Oral Lessons.*—Animals named in reading books.	Notation to 1,000. Coins and simple weights and measures. *Geography.* — The globe generally, size, zones, climate, races of men. *History.* — Oral lessons on States and Governments. *Elementary Physiology* and Hygiene. *Drawing* triangles and squares.	
Under 10. Standard III.	*Oral Exercises.* — Elementary grammar and analysis of sentences. Writing a letter. *Arithmetic.* — Reduction; simple fractions; interest. *Geography.*—The Northern States. *Music.* — Singing at sight in keys of C, G, D, and F. *Drawing.* — Combinations of square,	*Oral Exercises.*— Use of "who, which, and that." Letter writing, descriptions of objects and events. *Reading.* — Prose chiefly; spelling. *Arithmetic,* oral and written, with numbers up to 10,000. Simple fractions up to twelfths. *Weights* and time. *Geography.*— North	*Reading.* — Second book. *Writing* and *spelling* on slates and paper. *Numeration* to 1,000,000. *Multiplication* and division. *Local geography* and definitions. *Elements* of musical notation.

124　　NOTES ON AMERICAN SCHOOLS

SCHEMES OF GRADED INSTRUCTION IN PRIMARY

AGE.	ENGLAND.	NEW YORK.	PHILADELPHIA.
Under 10. Standard III.	with long division. Addition and subtraction of money. *To recite* with intelligence and expression 60 lines of poetry, and to know their meaning. *Sewing* (girls). *To point out* nouns, verbs, adjectives, adverbs, and personal pronouns, and to form simple sentences containing them. *Physical* and political geography of England, with special knowledge of the district in which the school is situated. *Or* Elementary science.	*Penmanship.*—Practice in capitals. *Drawing* from dictation and from chart. *Combination* of circles with rectilinear figures.	money, concrete illustrations of fractions. *Geography.*—Physical features. America. *Drawing and design* from copies and objects. *Lessons* on plants. Animals. The human body.
Under 11. Standard IV.	*To read* a few lines from a reading book, or History of England. *Eight lines* of poetry or prose, slowly read once, and then dictated. *Copybooks* to be shown. *Compound rules* (money) and reduction of com-	*Language.* — Reading (4th book); oral lessons on plants; composition, written and *oral.* Suffixes. *Arithmetic.* — Common fractions, with their applications. *Geography.*—America and Europe. *Penmanship.*—	*Reading.* — Accent, emphasis. Use of dictionary. Recitation. Copying letters, bills, accounts. Composition. Analysis of simple sentences. *Arithmetic.*—Measures, multiples, fractions. *Geography.*—Latitude, longitude, United States.

AND TRAINING COLLEGES. 125

SCHOOLS FOR CHILDREN FROM 6 TO 14—*Cont.*

AGE.	CHICAGO.	MASSACHUSETTS.	ONTARIO (FOUR STAGES).
Under 10. Standard III.	oblong, and equilateral triangles. *Cutting* out geometrical figures. *Oral Lessons.* —Personal habits. Conduct.	America. Physical and political. Sketch maps. *History.* — Local traditions, growth of cities, and of government. *Physiology.* — Parts of the body. The senses. *Drawing*.— The circle and its combinations, with rectilinear figures. Use of color.	*Oral* and written composition. *Object lessons.*
Under 11. Standard IV.	*Grammar.*— Composition, business terms, analysis, reading. *Arithmetic.*—Prime numbers, factors, measures and multiples, fractions. *Outline geography* of principal countries. *Singing* at sight in keys of C, G, D, F, and B flat.	*Recitation* of prose and verse. *Train*, orally and by dictation, in the right use of *sit, set, lie, lay, shall,* and *will*, and other words often misused. *Reading* and use of dictionary for meaning of new words. *Arithmetic.* — Deci-	

126   NOTES ON AMERICAN SCHOOLS

SCHEMES OF GRADED INSTRUCTION IN PRIMARY

AGE.	ENGLAND.	NEW YORK.	PHILADELPHIA.
Under 11. Standard IV.	mon weights and measures. *To recite* 80 lines of poetry, and to explain the words and allusions. *Sewing* and knitting (girls). *To parse* easy sentences, and to show by examples the use of each of the parts of speech. *Physical* and political geography of the British Isles, and of British North America or Australasia, with knowledge of their productions. *Or* Elementary science.	Short phrases and easy sentences. *Drawing.* — Elliptical and other curves; designs for borders, etc.	*History.* — Biography, oral lessons. *Science.*—Plants, hygiene. *Drawing.* — Geometrical, decorative, model, etc.
Under 12. Standard V.	*To read* a passage from some standard author, or from a History of England. *Writing* from memory the substance of a short story read out twice; spelling, handwriting, and correct expression to be considered. *Copybooks* to be shown. *Practice,* bills of par-	*Language.*—Reading, composition, prefixes and suffixes. English grammar (without text-book). Parts of speech. Subject, predicate, object. *Arithmetic.* — Former rules applied. *Geography.*—Review America, Asia and Africa in outline. *History* of United	*Reading* and recitation. Common prefixes and suffixes. Parsing and analysis. Business correspondence. *Arithmetic.* — Percentage, fractions, English money, computation of time, longitude, insurance, etc. *Geography.* — Europe, Asia, Africa. *History* of United

AND TRAINING COLLEGES. 127

SCHOOLS FOR CHILDREN FROM 6 TO 14—*Cont.*

AGE.	CHICAGO.	MASSACHUSETTS.	ONTARIO.
Under 11. Standard IV.	*Drawing* objects and patterns. *Cutting out* of geometric figures. *Oral Lessons.*—Conduct and habits.	mal fractions to three places, prime numbers and factors, simple mensuration of surfaces. *Geography.*—United States, with special study and map of Massachusetts. *Outline History* of United States. *Physiology.* — Food, air, exercise. *Drawing.*— Ellipse, oval, etc., in combination.	
Under 12. Standard V.	*Analysis* and synthesis of simple sentences. Parsing. Simple prefixes and affixes. *Composition.*—Writing business letters. *Arithmetic.* —Vulgar and decimal fractions; measurement of rectangular surfaces. *Geography.*— Illinois and neighboring States. New	*Form* compound and complex sentences. *Reading* poetry. Vocal drill. *Arithmetic.*— Multiplication and division of fractions. *Geography.*—British America and Mexico, Europe. Latitude, etc. *Physiology.* — The nutritive and digestive system.	*Reading* 3d book. *Spelling* with verbal distinctions. *Writing* business forms. *Arithmetic.*— Greatest common measure; reduction and compound rules. *Drawing.* *Geography* of North America. Map drawing.

NOTES ON AMERICAN SCHOOLS

SCHEMES OF GRADED INSTRUCTION IN PRIMARY

AGE.	ENGLAND.	NEW YORK.	PHILADELPHIA.
Under 12. Standard V.	cels, and single rule of three by the method of unity. *Addition* and subtraction of proper fractions, with denominators not exceeding 10. *To recite* 100 lines from some standard poet, and to explain the words and allusions. *To parse* and analyze simple sentences, and to know the method of forming English nouns, adjectives, and verbs from each other. *Sewing* and cutting out (girls). *Geography* of Europe, physical and political. Latitude and longitude. Day and night. The seasons. *Or* Elementary science, *or* History. *Map drawing.* *Two* specific subjects. *	States without text-book. *Penmanship.*— Large and small hand. *Drawing* and design. Patterns, ornaments, foliage, etc.	States, colonial period. *Science.*—Animal physiology and hygiene. *Constructive* and decorative drawing.

* In the Fifth Standard and upwards, teachers are at liberty to select two additional or specific subjects from a schedule, containing Mechanics, Geometry and Algebra, Animal Physiology, Botany, Domestic Economy, Elementary French, Latin, etc.

AND TRAINING COLLEGES. 129

SCHOOLS FOR CHILDREN FROM 6 TO 14—*Cont.*

AGE.	CHICAGO.	MASSACHUSETTS.	ONTARIO.
Under 12. Standard V.	England States; outline maps. *Physiology.* — H o w we live. *Part* and c h o r u s singing by note. *Drawing.* — Cutting patterns and design. *Oral Lessons.*—Habits, conduct, city government.	*Drawing.*— H e x a - gon, pentagon, octagon, design. Use of color. *Letter writing*, bills for merchandise and for service.	*Music* by note. *Words.*—Grammatical classification and inflection. *History.* — English and Canadian. *Oral Lessons.*—Animals and plants.

130 NOTES ON AMERICAN SCHOOLS

SCHEMES OF GRADED INSTRUCTION IN PRIMARY

AGE.	ENGLAND.	NEW YORK.	PHILADELPHIA.
Under 13. Standard VI.	*To read* a passage from one of Shakespeare's historical plays, or from some other standard author, or from a History of England. *A short theme* or letter on an easy subject; spelling, handwriting and composition to be considered. *Fractions,* vulgar and decimal; simple proportion and simple interest. *To recite* 150 lines from Shakespeare or Milton, or some other standard author, and to explain the words and allusions. *To parse* and analyze a short complex sentence, and to know the meaning and uses of Latin prefixes in the formation of English words. *Sewing* and cutting out (girls). *Geography* of the world generally, and especially of the British colonies and dependencies. Interchange of produc-	*Language.*—Reading, composition, formation of derivative words, grammar. *Arithmetic.*—Percentages and their application. *Geography.*—South America and Europe in detail. *History of United States* to the Revolution. *Penmanship.*—Letter writing. *Drawing* from dictation and from chart, ornamental designs, etc.	*Reading.*—Recitation, declamation, figures of speech, Latin prefixes and derivations. *Writing.*—Reproduction of stories and descriptions. Letter writing. Syntax and analysis. *Arithmetic.*—Discount, partnership, use of business terms, check, credit, debit, etc. *Geography.*—Australia. Special knowledge of State of Pennsylvania. *History.*—The American Revolution and Constitution. Civil war. *Elementary physics* and physiology. *Drawing,* constructive and inventive.

AND TRAINING COLLEGES. 131

SCHOOLS FOR CHILDREN FROM 6 TO 14—*Cont.*

AGE.	CHICAGO.	MASSACHUSETTS.	ONTARIO.
Under 13. Standard VI.	*Syntax*, paraphrase, and analysis. *Composition.*—Business forms. *Arithmetic.*—Commission, discount, insurance, import duties, etc. *Geography.*—Great Britain and Europe. Map drawing. *History* of United States. Washington. *Historical poems* read in connection. *Music* by note. Writing the seven scales. Part singing. *Drawing.*—Invention, etc., of patterns and ornaments. *Oral Lessons.*—Habits and conduct.	*Analysis* of sentences, subject, predicate, and their modifications. *Writing* and spelling. *Arithmetic.*—Compound numbers, weights and measures, percentages. *Geography.*—Asia, Africa, and Australia. Commerce of United States. *History* of America *Physiology.*—Circulatory and respiratory system. *Drawing* from spherical objects. Design using geometrical forms. Tinting.	

NOTES ON AMERICAN SCHOOLS

SCHEMES OF GRADED INSTRUCTION IN PRIMARY

AGE.	ENGLAND.	NEW YORK.	PHILADELPHIA.
Under 13. Standard VI.	tions. Circumstances which determine climate. *Or* Elementary science, *or* History. *Two* specific subjects.		
Under 14. Standard VII.	*To read* a passage from Shakespeare or Milton, or from some other standard author, or from a History of England. *A theme* or letter. Composition, spelling and handwriting to be considered. *Note-books* and exercise books to be shown. *Compound proportion*, averages, and percentages. *To recite* 150 lines from Shakespeare or Milton, or some other standard author, and to explain the words and allusions. *To analyze* sentences, and to know prefixes and terminations generally. *The ocean.* Currents and tides. General arrangement of the planetary system. The phases of the moon. *Or* Elementary science, *or* History. *Two* specific subjects.	*Language.* — Reading, meaning and use of words. Grammar. The formation of words from roots. *Arithmetic.* — Exchange, Custom House business, partnership, and mensuration. *Geography.* — General review, Constitution, and State Government. *Penmanship.*—Business forms; letters. *Drawing* on paper. Designs, etc. *Plane geometry* and perspective.	*Reading*, recitation, declamation. Prose and poetry versification. Derivation of words. *Writing* commercial forms and letters. Paraphrase and analysis. *Arithmetic.* — Powers of numbers, square root, mensuration. *Commercial geography*, sketch maps. *History.*—The Federal and State Constitutions. *Physiology and Physics* advanced. *Drawing* and design.

AND TRAINING COLLEGES.

SCHOOLS FOR CHILDREN FROM 6 TO 14—*Cont.*

AGE.	CHICAGO.	MASSACHUSETTS.	ONTARIO.
Under 13. Standard VI.			
Under 14. Standard VII.	*Grammar*, parsing, composition, oral composition on works read. *Arithmetic.*--Square root, measuration, stocks. *Longitude* and time. *Geography* in connection with history. *History* of the United States and England (in connection with settlement and growth of United States). *Physiology.* — How we live. *Music* by note, advanced. *Drawing.* — Perspective, etc. *Oral* lessons on conduct. American authors.	*Analysis* of compound sentences. Declamation. Oral and written composition. *Reading* in turn to the whole school. *Arithmetic.*—Ratio, proportion, interest, discount, and business forms. *Geography.*—Physical facts generally. *History.*--The Revolution. American Constitution, slavery, growth of industries. *Physiology.* — Hygiene: effect of stimulants, narcotics, etc. *Drawing* and design.	*Reading* 4th book. *Writing* business letters and accounts. *Drawing.* *Geography* of the world. Map drawing of Canada. *Arithmetic.* — Fractions, interest, percentage. *Grammatical parsing* and analysis. *English* and Canadian history.

"THE BEST EXISTING 'VADE MECUM' FOR THE TEACHER."

BY THE SAME AUTHOR.

LECTURES ON TEACHING,

Delivered in the University of Cambridge,

BY

J. G. FITCH, M.A.,

With Introductory Preface by THOMAS HUNTER, Ph.D., President of
the Normal College, New York.

16mo, Cloth. $1.00.

From the New England Journal of Education.

"This is eminently the work of a man of wisdom and experience.
He takes a broad and comprehensive view of the work of the teacher,
and his suggestions on all topics are worthy of the most careful consideration."

OTHER PRESS NOTICES.

"The lectures will be found most interesting, and deserve to be
carefully studied, not only by persons directly concerned with instruction, but by parents who wish to be able to exercise an intelligent
judgment in the choice of schools and teachers for their children. For
ourselves, we could almost wish to be of school age again, to learn
history and geography from some one who could teach them after the
pattern set by Mr. Fitch to his audience. But perhaps Mr. Fitch's ob-
observations on the general conditions of school work are even more
important than what he says on this or that branch of study."
—*Saturday Review.*

" It comprises fifteen lectures, dealing with such subjects as organization, discipline, examining, language, fact, knowledge, science, and
methods of instruction ; and though the lectures make no pretension
to systematic or exhaustive treatment, they yet leave very little of the
ground uncovered, and they combine in an admirable way the exposition of sound principles with the practical suggestions and illustrations
which are evidently derived from wide and varied experience, both in
teaching and examining."—*Scotsman.*

"As principal of a training college, and as a government inspector of
schools, Mr. Fitch has got at his fingers' ends the working of Primary
education, while as assistant commissioner to the late endowed schools
commission, he has seen something of the machinery of our higher
schools. . . . Mr. Fitch's book covers so wide a field, and touches
on so many burning questions, that we must be content to recommend it
as the best existing *vade mecum* for the teacher. He is always sensible,
always judicious, never wanting in tact. . . . Mr. Fitch is a scholar;
he pretends to no knowledge that he does not possess ; he brings to his
work the ripe experience of a well-stored mind, and he possesses in a
remarkable degree the art of exposition."—*Pall Mall Gazette.*

" Teachers, everywhere, are advised to make this excellent volume the
subject of careful and frequent study."—*School Journal.*

"A work which teachers cannot read too often or too thoroughly."
N. Y. Observer.

" To the teacher who has any sense of the value and importance of
his office, this must prove an invaluable volume. It will widen greatly
his view of the dignity and responsibility of the position he occupies,
and will offer him genuine and needed help in the performance of his
duties."—*Christian at Work.*

" The most valuable book of the kind that we know."—*Critic.*

" It is a book that will grace any teacher's shelf, and do him good
when he reads it."—*Educational News.*

" It is safe to say, no teacher can lay claim to being well informed
who has not read this admirable work. Its appreciation is shown by its
adoption by several State Teachers' Reading Circles, as a work to be
thoroughly read by its members."—*School Journal.*

" We are delighted with the new edition of Fitch's Lectures, and com-
mend it to all American teachers."—*Journal of Education.*

MACMILLAN & CO.'S
WORKS ON TEACHING, ETC.

BLAKISTON. The Teacher. Hints on School Management. A Handbook for Managers, Teachers, Assistants, and Pupil-Teachers. By J. R. BLAKISTON, M.A. (Recommended by the London, Birmingham, and Leicester School Boards.) 12mo. 75 cents.

"Into a comparatively small book he has crowded a great deal of exceedingly useful and sound advice. It is a plain, common-sense book, full of hints to the teacher on the management of his school and his children."—*School Board Chronicle.*

CALDERWOOD. On Teaching. By Professor HENRY CALDERWOOD, LL.D. New edition, with Chapter on Home Training, 12mo. 50 cents.

"For young teachers this work is of the highest value. . . . It is a book every teacher would find helpful in their responsible work."— *N. E. Journal of Education.*

"Here is a book which combines merits of the highest (and, alas! the rarest) order. . . . We have rarely met with anything on the subject of teaching which seems to us to appeal so directly both to the teacher's head and heart, and give him so clear an insight into the true nature of his calling."—*Monthly Journal of Education.*

COMBE. Education: Its Principles and Practice, as developed by GEORGE COMBE, author of "The Constitution of Man." Collated and Edited by Julius Jolly. 8vo. $5.00.

COMENIUS. John Amos Comenius. Bishop of the Moravians. His Life and Educational Works. By S. S. LAURIE, A.M., F.R.S.E. Second edition. Revised, 16mo. $1.00.

CRAIK. The State and Education. By HENRY CRAIK, M.A. 12mo. $1.00.

FEARON. School Inspection. By D. R. FEARON, M.A., Assistant Commissioner of Endowed Schools. New edition. 12mo. 75 cents.

FITCH. Lectures on Teaching. Delivered in the University of Cambridge. By J. G. FITCH, M.A., Her Majesty's Inspector of Schools. 12mo. American edition. $1.00.

GALTON. Inquiries into Human Faculty and its Development. By FRANCIS GALTON, F.R.S. Author of "Hereditary Genius," etc. With illustrations. 8vo. $3.00.

GEIKIE. The Teaching of Geography. Suggestions Regarding Principles and Methods for the Use of Teachers. By ARCHIBALD GEIKIE, LL.D., F.R.S. Director-General of the Geological Survey of the United Kingdom. 16mo. 60 cents.

GLADSTONE. Object Teaching. A Lecture delivered at the Pupil-Teacher Centre. By J. H. GLADSTONE, Ph.D., F.R.S. With an Appendix. 12mo. 10 cents.

"It is a short but interesting and instructive publication, and our younger teachers will do well to read it carefully and thoroughly. There is much in these few pages which they can learn and profit by." —*School Guardian.*

GLADSTONE. Spelling Reform, from an Educational Point of View. By J. H. GLADSTONE, F.R.S. Second edition. Enlarged 12mo. 50 cents.

LAURIE. Occasional Addresses on Educational Subjects. By S. S. LAURIE, A.M., LL.D., Professor of the Institute and History of Education in the University of Edinburgh. 12mo. $1.25.

"The whole lecture on this subject ought to be carefully read by American educators. . . . The whole book is very suggestive, and we trust will not be overlooked by any one interested in education."— *Science.*

LOCKE ON EDUCATION. With Introduction and Notes by the Rev. R. H. QUICK, M.A. 90 cents.

There is no teacher too young to find this book interesting ; there is no teacher too old to find it profitable."—*School Bulletin.*

LOCKE ON THE CONDUCT OF THE UNDERSTANDING. Edited, with Introduction and Notes, by T. FOWLER, M.A. 16mo. 50 cents.

" I cannot think any parent or instructor justified in neglecting to put this little treatise in the hands of a boy about the time when the reasoning faculties become developed."—*Hallam.*

MILTON'S TRACTATE ON EDUCATION. A fac-simile reprint from the edition of 1673. Edited, with Notes, by OSCAR BROWNING, M.A. 50 cents.

"We are grateful to Mr. Browning for his elegant and scholarly edition, to which is prefixed the careful *résumé* of the work given in his 'History of Educational Theories.'"—*Journal of Education.*

MORE'S UTOPIA. By Sir THOMAS MORE. Edited, with Notes by the Rev. Professor LUMBY. 16mo. 90 cents.

SWEET. A Primer of Phonetics. By HENRY SWEET, M.A., Balliol College, Oxford, Hon. Ph.D., Heidelberg. 16mo. 90 cents.

THREE LECTURES ON THE PRACTICE OF EDUCATION. Delivered in the University of Cambridge, in the Easter Term, 1882. 50 cents.
Contents : On Marking, by H. W. Eve, M.A. ; on Stimulus, by A. Sidgwick, M.A. ; on the Teaching of Latin Verse Composition, by E. A. Abbott, D.D.

" Like one of Bacon's Essays, it handles those things in which the writer's life is most conversant, and it will come home to men's business and bosoms. Like Bacon's Essays, too, it is full of apophthegms." —*Journal of Education.*

THRING. Theory and Practice of Teaching. By the Rev. EDWARD THRING, M.A. 16mo. Cambridge University Press. $1.00.

"We hope we have said enough to induce teachers in America to read Mr. Thring's book. They will find it a mine in which they will never dig without some substantial return, either in high inspiration or sound practical advice. Many of the hints and illustrations given are of the greatest value for the ordinary routine work of the class-room. Still more helpful will the book be found in the weapons which it furnishes to the schoolmaster wherewith to guard against his greatest danger— slavery to routine."—*Nation.*

Education and School. By the same author. Second edition. 12mo. $1.75.

TODHUNTER. The Conflict of Studies, and other Essays on Subjects Connected with Education. By I. TODHUNTER, M.A., F.R.S. 8vo. $2.50.

STANDARD BOOKS

ON THE STUDY

OF

THE ENGLISH LANGUAGE

AND LITERATURE.

·

PUBLISHED BY

MACMILLAN & CO.,

112 FOURTH AVENUE, NEW YORK.

CHAUCER'S
CANTERBURY TALES.

ANNOTATED AND ACCENTED

With Illustrations of English Life in Chaucer's Time.

BY

JOHN SAUNDERS.

With Illustrations from the Ellesmere MS.

12mo, $1.60.

CONTENTS:

Contemporary Men and Events of Chaucer's Period.
Introduction, showing the present Author's mode of dealing with the
Text.
The Prologue and Characters, with additional Illustrations of English
Life in the time of the Poet, in Six Sections, by the present Writer.

Section I.—THE TABARD.
Its History—A Visit to the Tabard.

Section II.—CHIVALRY.
The Knight—The Squire—The Yeoman.

Section III.—RELIGION.
The Religious Orders—The Monk—The Prioress—The Friar—
The Sumpnour—The Pardoner—The Parson.

Section IV.—PROFESSIONAL MEN.
The Sergeant-at-Law—The Manciple—The Doctor of Physic—
The Alchemist—The Clerk of Oxenford.

Section V.—TRADE AND COMMERCE.
Agriculture—The Franklin—The Miller—The Reeve—The Plough-
man.

Section VI.—TRADE AND COMMERCE (Continued).
The Merchant — The Shipman — The Haberdasher, etc. — The
Cook's Tale of the Prentice—The Cook—The Wife of Bath.

The Tales. The Knight's Tale—The Man of Law's Tale—The Wife
of Bath's Tale—The Friar's Tale—The Clerk's Tale—The Squire's
Tale—The Franklin's Tale—The Pardoner's Tale—The Prioress's
Tale—The Nun's Priest's Tale—The Second Nun's Tale—The
Canon's Yeoman's Tale—The Manciple's Tale—The Doctor's Tale.

Selections from the Other Tales. The Miller's Tale—The Reeve's
Tale—The Merchant's Tale—The Shipman's Tale.

NEW PUBLICATIONS.

CHAUCER. The Prologue, The Knightes Tale, The Nonne Preestes Tale, from the Canterbury Tales. Edited by the Rev. RICHARD MORRIS, LL.D. A new edition with Collations and additional Notes by the Rev. WALTER W. SKEAT, Litt.D. 16mo, 60 cents.

Prof. E. E. Hale, Jr., of Cornell, writes: "It is a great improvement over the original edition, which was in many ways the best book for a class beginning the study of Chaucer. The revised text is, of course, of the greatest value, and the corrections and additions by Prof. Skeat are, wherever I have compared the two editions, very much to the point."

CHAUCER. The Tale of the Man of Lawe. The Pardoneres Tale, The Second Nonnes Tale, The Chanouns Yemannes Tale, from The Canterbury Tales. Edited by the Rev. WALTER W. SKEAT, Litt.D., LL.D. New Edition, revised. 16mo, $1.10.

CHAUCER. The Prioresses Tale, Sire Thopas, The Monkes Tale, The Clerkes Tale, The Squieres Tale, from the Canterbury Tales. Edited by the Rev. WALTER W. SKEAT, Litt.D. Fourth Edition, revised. 16mo, $1.10.

"It would be hardly possible to find any pieces of English literature edited at any time more thoroughly for the help of students than these selections from Chaucer."—Professor H. MORLEY.

CHAUCER. The Legend of Good Women. Edited by the Rev. WALTER W. SKEAT, Litt.D. 12mo, $1.50.

"It is only a few months since Prof. Skeat published what is really the only existing critical edition of Chaucer's 'Minor Poems.' He has now performed the like service for the work which, next to the 'Canterbury Tales,' is the latest and ripest fruit of the poet's genius. Often as the 'Legend of Good Women' has been printed, it has never been edited until now. . . . Prof. Skeat's editions of the 'Minor Poems' and the 'Legend' form together a considerable instalment of the long-desired critical edition of Chaucer's poetry."—London Athenæum.

CHAUCER. The Minor Poems. Edited by the Rev. WALTER W. SKEAT, Litt.D., LL.D., Edin. ; M.A., Oxon. 12mo, $2.60.

"Professor Skeat has brought to bear upon the elucidation of the text all the great learning he has accumulated in the preparation of the various works with which his name is now so honorably connected. We have little hesitation in saying that there is no student of Chaucer living to whom this volume will not be an absolute necessity."
—*The Evening Post.*

"It contains a score of minor poems, which the editor, after skilled and diligent investigation, holds to be genuine. Our debt to Professor Skeat for giving us these poems in so accessible a form, and still more in so pure a text, cannot easily be overestimated."—*Literary World.*

LONGER ENGLISH POEMS.

With Notes Philological and Explanatory,

AND AN

Introduction on the Teaching of English.

EDITED BY

J. W. HALES, M.A.

16mo. $1.10.

CONTENTS.

PREFACE.—Suggestions on the Teaching of English.
SPENSER.—Prothalamion.
MILTON.—Hymn on the Nativity—L'Allegro—Il Penseroso
—Lycidas.
DRYDEN.—MacFlecknoe—A Song for St. Cecilia's Day—
Alexander's Feast; or, the Power of Music.
POPE.—Rape of the Lock.
JOHNSON.—London—The Vanity of Human Wishes.
COLLINS.—The Passions.
GRAY.—Elegy—The Progress of Poesy—The Bard.
GOLDSMITH.—The Traveller—The Deserted Village.
BURNS.—The Cotter's Saturday Night—The Twa Dogs.
COWPER.—Heroism—On the Receipt of my Mother's
Picture out of Norfolk.
SCOTT.—Cadyow Castle.
WORDSWORTH.—Ode : Imitations of Immortality from
Recollections of Early Childhood—Laodamia,
BYRON.—The Prisoner of Chillon.
KEATS.—The Eve of St. Agnes.
SHELLEY—Adonais.

"The Notes are very full and good, and the book, edited by one of our most cultivated English scholars, is probably the best volume of selections ever made for the use of English schools."—Professor MORLEY.

PUBLISHED SEPARATELY.

GOLDSMITH.—The Traveller and the Deserted Village.
With Notes Philological and Explanatory.
By J. W. HALES, M.A. 16mo. Stiff covers.
18 cents.

THE ENGLISH POETS

SELECTIONS.

WITH CRITICAL INTRODUCTIONS

BY VARIOUS WRITERS,

AND A GENERAL INTRODUCTION

BY

MATTHEW ARNOLD.

EDITED BY

THOMAS HUMPHRY WARD, M.A.

In Four Volumes. 12mo.
Cabinet Edition. Four Volumes in box, $5.00.
Student's Edition. Each volume sold separately, $1.00.
Vol. I.—Chaucer to Donne.
Vol. II.—Ben Jonson to Dryden.
Vol. III.—Addison to Blake.
Vol. IV.—Wordsworth to Rossetti.

"All lovers of poetry, all students of literature, all readers will welcome the volumes of 'The English Poets.' . . . Mr. Matthew Arnold has written a most delightful introduction, full of wise thought and poetic sensibility. . . . Very few books can be named in which so much that is precious can be had in so little space and for so little money."—*Philadelphia Times*.

"Altogether it would be difficult to select four volumes of any kind better worth owning and studying than these."—*Nation*.

"These four volumes ought to be placed in every library, and, if possible, in the hands of every student of English."—*Churchman*.

"The best collection ever made. . . . A nobler library of poetry and criticism is not to be found in the whole range of English literature."—*N. Y. Evening Mail*.

"For the young, no work they will meet with can give them so good a view of the large and rich inheritance that lies open to them in the poetry of their country."—J. C. SHAIRP, in *Academy*.

"I know of nothing more excellent or more indispensable than such a work, not only to the student of literature, but to the general reader. It is but simple justice to say that the book has no rival and is altogether unique."—Prof. ARTHUR H. DUNDON, Normal College, New York City.

"The sincere lovers of English poetry, in its successive stages of affluent development, will welcome this collection for the choice character of its contents, and the wise and pregnant body of criticism by various writers of note in English elegant literature which accompanies the original poems. Nothing of the kind has ever before been attempted on the scale of the present work, which is intended as a representative anthology of the wide field of English poetry."—*N. Y. Tribune*.

A HISTORY

OF

EIGHTEENTH CENTURY LITERATURE.

(1660–1780)

BY

EDMUND GOSSE, M.A.

Clark Lecturer in English Literature at Trinity College, Cambridge.

12mo. Cabinet Edition, $1.75; Student's Edition, $1.00.

CONTENTS.

Poetry after the Restoration.
Drama after the Restoration.
Prose after the Restoration.
Pope.
Swift and the Deists.
Defoe and the Essayists.
The Dawn of Naturalism in Poetry.
The Novelists.
Johnson and the Philosophers.
The Poets of the Decadence.
The Prose of the Decadence.
Conclusion—Bibliography—Index.

"The plan of the book is excellent. The central figures, around which the lesser writers are grouped, are well chosen and well treated. The mutual relations of the writers are clearly pointed out, and a due proportion is preserved in the space allotted to each. The tone is moderate, and the judgments free from exaggeration; while the connectedness of the book is well preserved throughout."—*The Educational Times.*

"Mr. Gosse's book is one for the student because of its fullness, its trustworthiness, and its thorough soundness of criticisms; and one for the general reader because of its pleasantness and interest. It is a book, indeed, not easy to put down or to part with."
—OSWAULD CRAWFORD, in *London Academy.*

"Mr. Gosse has in a sense preëmpted the eighteenth century. He is the most obvious person to write the history of its literature, and this attractive volume ought to be the final and standard work on his chosen theme."—*The Literary World.*

A HISTORY

OF

ELIZABETHAN LITERATURE.

BY

GEORGE SAINTSBURY.

12mo, Cabinet Edition, $1.75.   Student's Edition, $1.00.

CONTENTS:

From Tottel's Miscellany to Spenser.
Early Elizabethan Prose.
The First Dramatic Period.
"The Faërie Queene" and its Group.
The Second Dramatic Period—Shakespeare.
Later Elizabethan and Jacobean Prose.
The Third Dramatic Period.
The School of Spenser and the Tribe of Ben.
Milton, Taylor, Clarendon, Browne, Hobbes.
Caroline Poetry.
The Fourth Dramatic Period.
Minor Caroline Prose.

"Mr. Saintsbury has produced a most useful, first-hand survey—comprehensive, compendious, and spirited—of that unique period of literary history when 'all the muses still were in their prime.' One knows not where else to look for so well-proportioned and well-ordered conspectus of the astonishingly varied and rich products of the teeming English mind during the century that begins with Tottel's Miscellany and the birth of Bacon, and closes with the Restoration."—M. B. ANDERSON, in *The Dial*.

"Mr. Saintsbury's task was a particularly difficult one.   To have written an extended account of Elizabethan literature would have been much easier, for the abundance of material is an incentive to large treatment in such a case.   But to condense in one small volume the essence and gist of the most important prolific and impressive literary period in English history, if not in all history, calls for the exercise not only of rare discrimination, but also of a rare faculty of exposition.   .   .   . Regarding Mr. Saintsbury's work as a whole, we know not where else to find so compact, yet comprehensive, so judicious, weighty, and well written review and critique of Elizabethan literature.   .   .   .   But the analysis generally is eminently distinguished by insight, delicacy, and sound judgment, and this applies quite as much to the estimates of prose writers as to those of the poets and dramatists.   .   .   . a work which deserves to be styled admirable."—*New York Tribune*.

MACMILLAN & CO.

A SHAKESPEARIAN GRAMMAR. An attempt to illustrate some of the Differences between Elizabethan and Modern English. For the use of schools. By E. A. ABBOTT, D.D., Head Master of the City of London School. 16mo, $1.50.

"Valuable not only as an aid to the critical study of Shakespeare, but as tending to familiarize the reader with Elizabethan English in general."—*Athenæum*.

ELEMENTARY LESSONS IN HISTORICAL ENG-LISH GRAMMAR. Containing Accidence and Word-formation. New Edition. 18mo, 70 cents.

"Of Dr. Morris's qualification for the preparation of such a manual of instruction, there is no need to say a word ; there is probably not another English scholar living who is his superior, if his equal, in minute acquaintance with the historical development of our language. . . . . Dr. Morris, in this 'Historical Grammar,' has given us what must be the accepted class-book on this subject."—*New York Times*.

THE PHILOLOGY OF THE ENGLISH TONGUE. By JOHN EARLE, M.A., Professor of Anglo-Saxon in the University of Oxford. Fourth Edition, revised throughout and rewritten in part. *Clarendon Press Series.* 16mo, $1.75.

"Every page attests Mr. Earle's thorough knowledge of English in all its stages, and of the living Teutonic languages."—*Academy*.

ON THE STUDY OF WORDS. By RICHARD CHENE-VIX TRENCH, D.D., Archbishop. Twentieth Edition, revised by the Rev. A. L. MAYHEW. 16mo, $1.00.

AN ANGLO-SAXON PRIMER. With Grammar, Notes, and Glossary. By HENRY SWEET, M.A. Fourth Edition. *Clarendon Press Series.* 16mo, 60 cents.

"The whole of the Grammar is admirably and very carefully compiled. . . . The Glossary contains a large number of words, and supplies a sufficient Vocabulary for all that the beginner can want. . . . The book as it stands is marvelously compressed, and has been purposely brought within such a compass as allows it to be sold at a very moderate price."—Professor SKEAT, *in the Academy*.

AN ANGLO-SAXON READER. In Prose and Verse, with Grammatical Introduction, Notes, and Glossary. By HENRY SWEET, M.A. Sixth Edition, revised and enlarged. *Clarendon Press Series.* 16mo, $2.10.

"The Grammatical introduction will help students to master the difficulties even of Beowulf ; and a course through the Reader, with the help of the Glossary, will set students far on the way of being Anglo-Saxons."—*Notes and Queries*.

A SECOND ANGLO-SAXON READER. Archaic and Dialectal. By HENRY SWEET, M.A. *Clarendon Press Series.* 16mo, $1.10.

Macmillan & Co., Publishers, 112 Fourth Ave., New York.

STANDARD BOOKS

ON THE STUDY

OF THE

GREEK AND LATIN
LANGUAGES.

.

Correspondence from professors and teachers of the Classical Languages, regarding specimen copies and terms for introduction, respectfully invited. Send address for Catalogue to

MACMILLAN & CO., Publishers,

112 Fourth Avenue, New York.

THE ATTIC THEATRE.

A description of the Stage and Theatre of the Athenians, and of the Dramatic Performances at Athens.

BY

A. E. HAIGH, M.A.,

Late Fellow of Hertford, and Classical Lecturer at Corpus Christi and Wadham Colleges, Oxford.

With Facsimiles and Illustrations.

8vo, $3.00.

CONTENTS:

DRAMATIC CONTESTS AT ATHENS—THE PRODUCTION OF A PLAY—THE THEATRE—THE SCENERY—THE ACTORS —THE CHORUS—THE AUDIENCE.

"My purpose in this book has been to write a history of the Attic Drama from the theatrical, as opposed to the literary, point of view. The subject is one which has been practically revolutionized during the last half century, especially owing to the rich discoveries of inscriptions relating to theatrical affairs and the information supplied by excavations in the old Greek theatres. But, in spite of the copious accession of fresh materials, it is now more than fifty years since any work has appeared in English in which this particular department of Greek dramatic history has been treated in a comprehensive manner. The neglect is all the more remarkable, as the subject is undeniably of great interest and importance. In the first place, it is difficult to understand and appreciate the peculiar qualities of the existing Greek plays without acquiring some knowledge of the circumstances under which they were produced, and the limitations within which the ancient dramatic poets had to work. In the second place, the Attic drama was essentially a public institution, and formed one of the most conspicuous elements in the national life ; the various details connected with its management are incidentally most instructive, because of the curious lights which they throw upon the habits, feelings, and tastes of the old Athenians. It is owing to these several considerations that the present work has been undertaken."—*From the Preface.*

"A book more thorough and more trustworthy can seldom have been issued by the Clarendon Press.' It is unlikely that for a long time to come so good a book as the present will be superseded."—*The Academy.*

" Mr. Haigh's acute and laborious work is a substantive contribution to Greek Archæology and a very creditable example of English scholarship."—*St. James Gazette.*

A COMPANION
TO
SCHOOL CLASSICS.
BY
JAMES GOW, M.A., Litt. D.
Head Master of the High School, Nottingham.   Late Fellow of Trinity
College, Cambridge.

Second Edition, Revised. With Illustrations.

12mo, $1.75.

"By 'school classics' I mean classics with commentaries for use in
schools, and by describing the book as a 'companion' to these, I mean
that it attempts to give the information which a commentator is, from
the nature of his task, compelled to assume even in a young student.
My aim is to place before a young student a nucleus of well-ordered
knowledge, to which he is to add intelligent notes and illustrations
from his daily reading."—*From the Preface.*

CONTENTS:

A. **Classical Texts.** The Greek Alphabet—The Latin Alphabet—
Books and their Publication—The History of Classical Manuscripts
—Modern Libraries of Classical MSS.—Apparatus Critici—Textual
Criticism—Famous Scholars—Dialects and Pronunciation.

B. **Greece.** Greek Chronology—Greek Metrology—History of Athenian Government—Population of Attica—The Athenian Officials—
Athenian Deliberative Assemblies—The Athenian Army and Fleet
—Athenian Legal Procedure—Athenian Finance—Sparta—Colonies
and Cleruchies.

C. **Rome.** Roman Chronology—Roman Metrology—History of Ro-
man Government—Rome under the Kings—The Republic of Rome
—Characteristics of Magistracy—Religious Functionaries—Delib-
erative Assemblies—Classes of the Free People—Government of
Italy and the Provinces—The Imperial Government—The Roman
Army—Navy—Law—Finance.

D. **Drama.** The Greek Drama—The Roman Drama.

E. **Philosophy.** INDEX. Greek Index—Latin Index, and English
Index of Subjects.

"Mr. Gow has presented a vast amount of information in a small
compass; yet it is so well arranged, and so clearly stated, that, notwithstanding its condensation, it is read with ease and pleasure. Indeed,
we do not know where to look for so good an account of Athenian and
Roman public affairs in a form at once clear, concise, and full enough
for ordinary students as Mr. Gow has here given us."—*Science.*

"He has made use of the most recent authorities, and the young
student will find the pith of many books in the space of less than 400
pages. . . . .   Much of the information would be sought to no purpose in the ordinary manuals, and what is given is conveyed in its true
connection."—*Nation.*

"Excellently planned and admirably executed. The author—for
Mr. Gow is more than a compiler—has had a distinct object in view.
He is a distinguished student of the classics, and he is an eminent practical teacher. With such qualifications, we turn with confidence to a
reliable book."—*Educational Times.*

GREEK VERBS,
IRREGULAR AND DEFECTIVE :
Their Forms, Meaning, and Quantity.
EMBRACING ALL THE TENSES USED BY THE GREEK WRITERS,
With References to the Passages in which they are Found.

BY

WILLIAM VEITCH, LL.D., Edin.
New Edition. 12mo, $2.60.

The chief peculiarities which distinguish this book from others on the same subject are the following :

"*First.* The history of the verb is more fully developed by being traced to a later period of the language, and the prose usage given commensurately with the poetic. This fuller development will be of no slight advantage to the advanced scholar ; and I have taken care to prevent its proving injurious to the less advanced by marking as late those parts and forms which are not found in the purer writers.

"*Second.* I have enlarged considerably the list of verbs, and given anthority for every part for which authority could be found, for the present as well as for the derivative tenses.

"*Third.* And what I hold as capital importance—I have always given the parts in the simple form when I could find them, and in no instance have I given a compound without warning, or exhibiting its composition."—*From the Author's Preface.*

A Hand-Book to Modern Greek.
BY
EDGAR VINCENT and T. G. DICKSON.
Second Edition. Revised and Enlarged.

With an Introduction by **JOHN STUART BLACKIE,**
And an Appendix by **R. C. JEBB,**
On **"The Relation of Modern to Classical Greek,
Especially in Regard to Syntax."**
12mo, $1.60.

"In its present condition, Modern Greek is of the greatest interest to the classical student and the philologist, but hitherto it has been strangely neglected; few, even among professed scholars, are aware how small the difference is between the Greek of the New Testament and the Greek of a contemporary Athenian newspaper."—*Author's Preface.*

CONTENTS.

PART I. Grammar.
PART II. Dialogues—Letters.
PART III. Passages from Ancient Greek Authors, with Translations in Modern Greek.
PART IV. Selections from Contemporary Greek Writers.
PART V. Vocabnlary—The Written Character.
APPENDIX. By Prof. R. C. JEBB.

THE STUDENT'S CICERO.

ADAPTED FROM THE GERMAN OF DR. MUNK'S "GESCHICHTE DER
RÖMISCHEN LITERATUR."

BY THE

Rev. W. Y. FAUSSET, M.A.,

With a frontispiece portrait. 12mo, $1.00.

"This little book is a translation of the section devoted to Cicero in
the first volume of Dr. Munk's *Geschichte der Römischen Literatur*. It
is a literary biography of the great master of Latin prose, who wielded
his eloquence in a Rome which, in spite of Greek influences and a
tottering Republic, was still Rome, and free.

"I have adhered to the text as closely as possible; save that it seemed
well in the case of the large extracts from the Latin to go direct to the
originals. For the notes I am alone responsible."
—W. Y. FAUSSET, *in the Preface*.

"Eminently the sort of book that a student will find profitable and
stimulating."—*Spectator*.

THE ISLANDS OF THE AEGEAN.

BY THE

Rev. HENRY FANSHAWE TOZER, M.A., F.R.G.S.,

Fellow and Tutor of Exeter College, Oxford.

With Maps, etc. 12mo, cloth, $2.25.

The following islands were visited : Delos, Rheneia, and
Tenos; Crete; Naxos, Ios, and Sikinos; Santorin, Anti-
paros, and Paros; Lesbos; Chios; Samos; Patmos;
Rhodes; Lemnos; Thasos; Samothrace.

THE

ANCIENT CLASSICAL DRAMA :

A Study in Literary Evolution.

INTENDED FOR READERS IN ENGLISH, AND IN THE ORIGINAL.

BY

RICHARD G. MOULTON, M.A.,

Late Scholar of Christ's College, Cambridge University (Extension);
Lecturer in Literature; Author of "Shakespeare
as a Dramatic Artist."

12mo, $2.25.

THE PRINCIPLES OF SOUND AND INFLEXION

AS ILLUSTRATED IN THE

GREEK AND LATIN LANGUAGES.

BY

J. E. KING, M.A.,

Fellow and Tutor of Lincoln College, Oxford,

AND

C. COOKSON, M.A.,

Late Scholar of Corpus Christi College, Oxford; Assistant Master at St. Paul's School, London.

8vo, $4.50.

CONTENTS:

Part I.—PHONOLOGY.
Introduction—The Indo-European Languages—Sounds and their Classification—The Simple Vowel-Sounds—Diphthongs and Semi-Vowels—The Gutturals—The Dental, Labial, Liquid, and Nasal Consonants—The Spirants—Combinations of Sounds—Ablant or Vowel-gradation—Accent.

Part II.—MORPHOLOGY.
Nominal Inflexion—Pronominal Inflexion—Comparison of Adjectives-Numerals—The Verb.

Appendix I.—The two Degrees of the Reduced Root.
Appendix II.—Vowel-gradation in Nominal and Verbal Formations.
Index to Greek Words.
Index to Latin Words.

"Our authors have carried out their task with full competence, sound judgment, and great accuracy. There are abundant signs of independent study, and it would be superfluous to praise the general accuracy of the work. It is sure to find wide acceptance as an authoritative text-book."
—*Academy.*

JUST PUBLISHED.

AN INTRODUCTION

TO THE

COMPARATIVE GRAMMAR of GREEK and LATIN

BY

J. E. KING, M.A.,

Fellow and Tutor of Lincoln College, Oxford,

AND

C. COOKSON, M.A.,

Late Scholar of Corpus Christi College, Oxford; Assistant Master at St. Paul's School, London.

12mo, $1.40.

NEW PUBLICATIONS.   7

MACMILLAN'S CLASSICAL SERIES

FOR COLLEGES AND SCHOOLS.

RECENT VOLUMES.

DEMOSTHENES. De Corona. Edited, with Introduction and Notes, by B. DRAKE, Late Fellow of King's College, Cambridge. Seventh Edition. revised and enlarged. Edited by E. S. SHUCK-BURGH, M.A. 16mo, $1.00.

"In this (seventh) issue of the late Mr. Drake's popular edition of the *De Corona*, the text has been revised, the Notes in part re-written, about a third additional matter inserted, and the Index expanded so as to give fuller references to words and phrases, and a complete monasticon of the Oration."—MR. E. S. SHUCKBURGH, *in the Preface.*

JUVENAL. The Thirteen Satires of Juvenal. Edited for the use of Schools, with Notes, Introductions, and Appendices, by E. G. HARDY, M.A., Head-Master of the Grammar School, Grantham, Late Fellow of Jesus College, Oxford. 16mo, $1.25.

LIVY. Books XXI. and XXII. Hannibals First Campaign in Italy. Edited, with Introductions, Notes, Appendices, and Maps, by the Rev. W. W. CAPES. Fellow of Hertford College, and Reader in Ancient History, Oxford. 16mo, $1.10.

"Equally distinguished for scholarship and common sense. Help of all kinds is plentifully but judiciously given, and there are few Latin scholars who could peruse the work without learning much."—*Athenæum.*

LYSIAS. Select Orations. With Analysis, Notes, Appendices, and Indices, by EVELYN S. SHUCKBURGH, M.A., Late Assistant-Master at Eton; formerly Fellow and Assistant-Tutor of Emmanuel College, Cambridge. New Edition, revised. 16mo, $1.60.

"Having read Mr. Shuckburgh's book and examined it minutely from beginning to end, I wish to say that, in my opinion, it is an admirable, scholarly piece of work in its kind, and beyond all doubt the most important help to the school study of Lysias which has yet appeared in this country."—Prof. JEBB, in the *Academy.*

PLATO. The Republic of Plato. Books I. to V. With Introduction and Notes, by T. HERBERT WARREN, M.A., President of St. Mary Magdalen College, Oxford. 16mo, $1.50.

This is the first commentary in English on so many as five books of the Republic. The Introduction deals with (1) The Name and Aim of the *Republic;* (2) The System of Education in the *Republic;* (3) The *Dramatis Personæ* of the *Republic.*

PLINY. Letters. Books I. and II. With Introduction, Notes, and Plan. Edited by JAMES COWAN, M.A. 16mo, $1.10.

Pliny's letters have hitherto been known to school-boys chiefly by selections. The Notes have been written chiefly for the higher forms in schools, but they will, it is hoped, be found sufficiently advanced for students at the University.

TACITUS. The Histories. Books III., IV., and V. With Introduction and Notes, by A. D. GODLEY, M.A. 16mo, $1.25.

MACMILLAN'S ELEMENTARY CLASSICS.

RECENT VOLUMES.

18mo, 40 cents each.

CAESAR. The Helvetian War. Being Selections from Book I. of the " De Bello Gallico." Adapted for the use of Beginners. With Notes, Exercises, and Vocabulary, by W. WELCH, M.A., and C. G. DUFFIELD, M.A.

CAESAR. The Invasion of Britain. Being Selections from Books IV. and V., of the " De Bello Gallico." Adapted for the use of Beginners. With Notes, Exercises, and Vocabulary, by W. WELCH, M.A., and C. G. DUFFIELD, M.A.

CICERO. De Senectute. Edited for the use of Schools. With Notes, Vocabulary, and Biographical Index, by E. S. SHUCKBURGH, M.A., Late Fellow of Emmanuel College, Cambridge.

"A thorough piece of work, showing not only sound scholarship, but taste and judgment."—*Journal of Education.*

CICERO. Stories of Roman History. Adapted for the use of Beginners. With Notes, Vocabulary, and Exercises, by the Rev. G. E. JEANS, Fellow of Hertford College, Oxford, and A. V. JONES, M.A., Assistant-Masters at Haileybury College.

" A very easy and interesting construing and exercise book for beginners, with excellent notes, introductions, and a vocabulary, which saves the use and expense of a dictionary."—*School Board Chronicle.*

HOMER. Iliad. Book I. Edited, for the use of Schools, by the Rev. JOHN BOND, M.A., and A. S. WALPOLE, M.A. With Notes and Vocabulary.

HOMER. Odyssey. Book I. Edited, for the use of Schools, by the Rev. JOHN BOND, M.A., and A. S. WALPOLE, M.A. With Notes and Vocabulary.

LIVY. Book I. Edited, with Notes and Vocabulary, for the use of Schools, by H. M. STEPHENSON, M.A., Late Head-Master of St. Peter's School, York.

LIVY. Legends of Early Rome. Adapted for the use of Beginners. With Notes, Exercises, and Vocabulary, by HERBERT WILKINSON, M.A.

NEPOS. Selections Illustrative of Greek and Roman History. Edited for the use of Beginners. With Notes, Vocabulary, and Exercises, by G. S. FARNELL, M.A.

" At once the handiest and best prepared edition for the use of beginners that we remember to have seen."—*Science.*

VIRGIL. Georgics I. Edited, with Notes and Vocabulary, by T. E. PAGE, M.A., Assistant-Master at the Charterhouse.

XENOPHON. Anabasis. Book I. Edited for the use of Schools, by A. S. WALPOLE, M.A., formerly Scholar of Worcester College, Oxford. With Notes, Vocabulary, and Illustrations.

NEW PUBLICATIONS. 9

Clarendon Press Series.

RECENT VOLUMES.

16mo.

CICERO. **Select Letters of Cicero.** With Notes, for the use of Schools, by the late CONSTANTINE E. PRICHARD, M.A., formerly Fellow of Balliol College, and EDWARD R. BERNARD, M.A., Fellow of Magdalen College. Second Edition. 16mo, 75 cents.

HOMER. **Iliad. Books I.–XII.** With an Introduction, a brief Homeric Grammar, and Notes, by D. B. MONRO, M.A., Provost of Oriel College, Oxford. Third Edition, Revised. 16mo, $1.50.

"As a school book it could hardly be excelled."
—*Journal of Education.*

"Certainly the best school edition of any portion of the works of Homer that has come under our notice."—*Saturday Review.*

HOMER. **Iliad. Books XIII.–XXIV.** With Notes by D. B. MONRO, M.A. 16mo, $1.50.

HOMER. **Odyssey. Books I.–XII.** With Introduction, Notes, etc., by W. W. MERRY, Rector of Lincoln College, Oxford. Fifty-fifth thousand. Carefully Revised. 16mo, $1.10.

HOMER. **Odyssey. Books XIII.–XXIV.** With Introduction, Notes, etc., by W. W. MERRY, M.A. Third Edition. 16mo, $1.10.

HORACE. **The Odes, Carmen Seculare, and Epodes.** With a Commentary by E. C. WICKHAM, M.A., Master of Wellington College, and late Fellow of New College, Oxford. New Edition, Revised. 16mo, $1.40.

PLINY. **Selected Letters of Pliny.** With Notes, for the use of Schools, by the late CONSTANTINE E. PRICHARD, M.A., formerly Fellow of Balliol College, and EDWARD R. BERNARD, M.A., formerly fellow of Magdalen College. Third Edition, Revised. 75 cents.

EURIPIDES. **Hecuba.** Edited, with Introduction and Notes, by CECIL H. RUSSELL, M.A., Assistant-Master at Clifton College; late Scholar of Trinity College, Oxford. 60 cents.

TACITUS. **The Annals of Tacitus. Books I.–IV.** Edited, with Introduction and Notes, for the use of Schools and Junior Students, by H. FURNEAUX, M.A., formerly Fellow and Tutor of Corpus Christi College, Oxford. $1.25.

PITT PRESS SERIES.

RECENT VOLUMES.

16mo.

CICERO. Oratio Pro Archia Poeta. Edited for Schools and Colleges by JAMES S. REID, Litt.D., Fellow and Tutor of Gonville and Caius College, Cambridge. New Edition, with corrections and additions. 50 cents.

"It is an admirable specimen of careful editing. . . . No boy can master this little volume without feeling that he has advanced a long step in scholarship."—*Academy.*

EURIPIDES. Iphigenia at Aulis of Euripides. With Introduction and Notes by CLINTON E. S. HEADLAM, B.A., Fellow of Trinity Hall, Cambridge. 65 cents.

PLATO. Crito. With Introduction, Notes, and Appendix, by J. ADAM, B.A., Fellow and Classical Lecturer of Emmanuel College, Cambridge. 60 cents.

"A most thorough piece of work, representing throughout the latest results of scholarship, and containing at the same time a good deal of original matter."—*Educational Times.*

PLUTARCH. Life of Timoleon. With Introduction, Notes, Maps, and Lexicon, by the Rev. HUBERT A. HOLDEN, M.A., LL.D., Examiner in Greek to the University of London, Sometime Fellow of Trinity College, Cambridge. $1.50.

PLUTARCH. Life of Nikias. With Introduction, Notes, and Lexicon, by the Rev. HUBERT A. HOLDEN, M.A., LL.D., Examiner in Greek to the University of London, sometime Fellow of Trinity College, Cambridge. $1.25.

SOPHOCLES. Oedipus Tyrannus. Edited by R. C. JEBB, Professor of Greek in the University of Glasgow, formerly Fellow of Trinity College and Public Orator in the University of Cambridge. $1.10.

VIRGIL. Bucolics. Edited with Introduction and English Notes by A. SIDGWICK, M.A., Fellow and Tutor of Corpus Christi, Oxford. 40 cents.

XENOPHON. Cyropaedia. Books I. and II. With Introduction and Notes, by the Rev. HUBERT A. HOLDEN, M.A., LL.D., Examiner in Greek to the University of London, Sometime Fellow of Trinity College, Cambridge.

  Part I. Introduction and Text.
  Part II. Notes, Critical Appendix, and Indices.
  The two parts, $1.50.

GREEK TESTAMENTS.

THE NEW TESTAMENT IN THE ORIGINAL GREEK. The text revised by BROOKE FOSS WESTCOTT, D.D., and FENTON JOHN ANTHONY HORT, D.D. 18mo, cloth, $1.00; leather, $1.25.

Students' Edition of the above, with **Greek-English Lexicon,** in strong leather binding, $1.90.

THE ACTS OF THE APOSTLES. Being the Greek text as revised by Drs. WESTCOTT and HORT, with Explanatory Notes by THOMAS ETHELBERT PAGE, M.A., Assistant-Master at Charter house, and formerly Fellow of St. John's College, Cambridge. 16mo, $1.10.

SCHOOL READINGS IN THE GREEK TESTAMENT. Being the outline of the Life of our Lord as given by ST. MARK, with additions from the text of the other Evangelists. Arranged and Edited, with Notes and Vocabulary, by ARTHUR CALVERT, M.A., Late Fellow of St. John's College, Cambridge. 16mo, $1.10.

A GREEK TESTAMENT PRIMER. An Easy Grammar and Reading Book for the use of students beginning Greek. By the Rev. EDWARD MILLER, M.A., Rector of Bucknell. 16mo, 90 cents.

GREEK TESTAMENT. ST. MATTHEW. By the Rev. A. SLOMAN, M.A., formerly Master at Westminster; Head-Master of Birkenhead School. 16mo, 60 cents.

This edition, which is uniform with Mr. Page's edition of *The Acts of the Apostles*, is an attempt to supply to the average school-boy the necessary help and materials for reading the Greek text of St. Matthew intelligently. Few boys will read long notes. Accordingly brevity has been studied as far as is consistent with clearness. The Greek text is that of Westcott and Hort.

THE CAMBRIDGE GREEK TESTAMENT FOR SCHOOLS AND COLLEGES. With a revised text and English Notes. Prepared under the direction of J. J. S. PEROWNE, D.D., Dean of Peterborough.

Gospel according to St. Matthew. By Rev. A. CARR. With Maps. $1.10.

Gospel according to St. Mark. By Rev. G. F. MACLEAR. With Maps. $1.10.

Gospel according to St. Luke. By Archdeacon FARRAR. With 4 Maps. $1.50.

Gospel according to St. John. By Rev. A. PLUMMER, M.A. With 4 Maps. $1.50.

Acts of the Apostles. By Rev. Professor LUMBY, D.D. With 4 Maps. $1.50.

First Epistle to the Corinthians. By Rev. J. J. LIAS. With Maps. 75 cents.

Epistles of St. John. By Rev. A. PLUMMER, M.A., D.D. $1.00.

Epistle to the Hebrews. By Archdeacon FARRAR, D.D. 90 cents.

TRANSLATIONS OF THE CLASSICS.

HERODOTUS. The History of Herodotus. Translated into English, with Notes, by G. C. MACAULAY, M.A., formerly of Trinity College, Cambridge. 2 vols., 12mo, $4.50.

HOMER. The Iliad of Homer done into English Prose, by ANDREW LANG, M.A., WALTER LEAF, M.A., and ERNEST MYERS, M.A. 12mo, $1.50.
"This work is a fruit of the ripest English scholarship. It represents ample learning, and it is pervaded by that intellectual sympathy which puts a translator into the atmosphere of another age, and into the thoughts of another man."—*Christian Union.*

HOMER. The Odyssey of Homer done into English Prose, by S. H. BUTCHER, M.A., Fellow and Prœlector of University College, Oxford, and A. LANG, M.A., late Fellow of Merton College, Oxford. Third Edition, revised and corrected. With additional Notes. 12mo, $1.50.
"The present brilliant translation of the Odyssey is another most gratifying proof of the taste and soundness of English scholarship."
—*Saturday Review.*
"Certainly no verse translation that we have yet read can carry one through the poem with so much interest, and so little sense of monotony."—*Nation.*
The above two volumes can also be had bound in cloth, uniform, with gilt top, in paper box. Price, $3.00.

HORACE. The Works of Horace. Rendered into English Prose. With Introductions, Running Analysis, Notes, and Index, by JAMES LONSDALE, M.A., and SAMUEL LEE, M.A. *Globe Edition.* $1.25.
"To classical and non-classical readers it will be invaluable."
—*London Standard.*

POLYBIUS. The Histories of Polybius. Translated from the text of F. HULTSCH by E. S. SHUCKBURGH, M.A., late Fellow of Emmanuel College, Cambridge. 2 vols., Post 8vo, $6.00.
"Is what all who know Mr. Shuckburgh's sound and varied scholarship would be led to expect."—*Nation.*
"The first English translation of the complete works of Polybius, so far as they are now known, . . . a painstaking and excellent piece of work, . . . in good and agreeable English."—*The Academy.*
"This is the first full translation of the historian that has been made into English, and the thoroughness with which the labor has been carried through will do honor both to its author and to English scholarship."—*Scotsman.*

VIRGIL. The Works of Virgil. Rendered into English Prose, with Introductions, Notes, Running Analysis, and an Index, by JAMES LONSDALE, M.A., and SAMUEL LEE, M.A. *Globe Edition.* $1.25.
"A more complete edition of Virgil in English it is scarcely possible to conceive than the scholarly work before us."—*Globe.*

XENOPHON. The Works of Xenophon. Translated into English, with Introduction and Notes, by H. G. DAKYNS, M.A. 12mo. Vol. I. $2.50.
.*. *Will be completed in 4 volumes.*

Macmillan & Co., 112 Fourth Ave., New York.

www.ingramcontent.com/pod-product-compliance
Lightning Source LLC
Chambersburg PA
CBHW030310170426
43202CB00009B/940